Artificial Intelligence and the Rule of Law

Artificial intelligence is an important driving force of the new round of technological revolution and industrial change. Artificial intelligence and blockchain have risen to the level of national policy. While the rapid development of AI brings convenience to people's lives, it also poses challenges to global changes and the development of human society, social governance and legal regulation, such as the leakage of personal privacy, frequent data security problems, and prejudice and discrimination caused by algorithms. AI is profoundly changing the world, and it is necessary to think about how to promote the construction of responsible AI from the perspective of global governance in the future.

In response to these issues, this series aims to explore and study the new situations and new issues at the intersection of AI, law and political science all over the world, to provide a legal basis for the development of AI-related frontier fields and to limit the development of AI within the framework of law to promote the harmonious and orderly construction of AI and legal systems. Based on the above purpose, this series is selected and integrated with multidisciplinary strengths to strengthen the research on legal, ethical, and social issues related to AI, focusing on laws, regulations, institutional systems, and ethics for the healthy development of AI. The authors of this series are all top authoritative experts and scholars in AI, law, political science, and other disciplines in China, and they have already made considerable achievements and social reputations in this field of research.

This series has a clear awareness of the problem and proposes specific solutions for the implementation and implementation of AI governance from a multidisciplinary and multidisciplinary perspective, covering AI, blockchain, algorithms, digital currency and other specific segments closely related to law, with cutting-edge, academic and theoretical value, and filling the gap of similar research in China.

Shuhong Zhao

Principle of Criminal Imputation for Negligence Crime Involving Artificial Intelligence

Springer

Shuhong Zhao
College for Criminal Law Science
Beijing Normal University
Beijing, China

ISSN 2731-6238 ISSN 2731-6246 (electronic)
Artificial Intelligence and the Rule of Law
ISBN 978-981-97-0721-8 ISBN 978-981-97-0722-5 (eBook)
https://doi.org/10.1007/978-981-97-0722-5

This Springer imprint is published by the registered company Springer Nature Singapore Pte Ltd.
The registered company address is: 152 Beach Road, #21-01/04 Gateway East, Singapore 189721, Singapore

Preface

In this day and age, with the wide application of Artificial Intelligence (AI) affecting our interaction and decision-making in new ways, AI has had a profound and dynamic impact on our society, and human life and human thought, in both positive and negative ways. There is no doubt that AI has become a constitutive element of our human society. While AI technology can be of great service to humanity and all countries can benefit from it, it likewise raises fundamental ethical concerns, such as the possibility that AI technology may exacerbate prejudice and may lead to discrimination, inequality, and the digital divide, creating a social or economic divide. This undoubtedly brings various potential impacts and challenges to human dignity, human rights and fundamental freedoms, as well as society and culture.

Specifically in the field of criminal law, due to the fact that the crime involving AI is different from the traditional one in terms of its actus reus, result and subject, the biggest challenge brought by the crime involving AI to criminal law theory and judicial practice is how to reasonably attribute responsibility to the perpetrator, especially in the negligence crime involving AI. To address this challenge, this study attempts to provide a rational theoretical framework for the imputation for such crime involving AI. Therefore, the discussion on the principle of imputation for such crime is at the core of this study. To this end, the logic and content of the corresponding arguments are elaborated and developed in the following chapters of this book.

The understanding of crime involving AI presupposes a sound definition of AI. While defining it needs to change over time, in accordance with technological developments, a description of the characteristics of AI is helpful in understanding AI. According to the general understanding, an AI system is a system that has the ability to process data and information in a way that resembles intelligent behavior and usually includes reasoning, learning, perception, prediction, planning, or control. Thus, AI is generally considered to be characterized by the following four aspects: deep learning, cross-border integration, Human-in-the-Loop, and Openness to swarm-intelligence. In this context, crimes involving AI are mainly crimes committed by using AI and the crimes caused by AI failing to fulfill its obligations to produce and manage safely. The first one of these two crimes is an intentional crime, while the second is a crime of negligence. Such descriptions, which are carried out in Chap. 1, provide a basic premise for this study.

Since the crime involving AI differs from the traditional one in its characteristics, what challenge does the traditional imputation theory face in attributing responsibility to the perpetrator in this kind of crime? The question is elaborated in Chap. 1, with the fundamental aim of identifying the core issues that this study attempts to address. In this type of negligence crime, because the application of AI technology has made great changes in the foreseeability, causality, duty of care and the imputation structure, it creates the gaps in the imputation for the negligence crime involving AI. Such criminal imputation gaps may cause the perpetrator that should bear criminal responsibility to escape his responsibility, while the perpetrator that do not need to bear such responsibility bears certain responsibility. The imputation gaps have no possibility to arise in the intentional crimes committed using AI. In this type of crime, because the attributes of the AI product as a criminal tool have not changed, the mistake theory in the criminal law can completely achieve the reasonable imputation for the crimes. Therefore, the theoretical challenges to the criminal imputation are mainly found in the negligence crime involving AI.

In response to such criminal imputation gaps, Chap. 2 of this study focuses on the theoretical premises for the reasonable imputation for negligence crime involving AI. To this end, one direction of such effort is to stipulate the principle of strict liability as well as new AI-related crimes such as the crime of malicious use of AI; and another attempt is to advocate the establishment of a specific AI criminal law system in terms of the subject of the crime, actus reus, and the penal system. However, instead of solving the problem of gaps in the criminal imputation, these legislative efforts have created the new challenges to the stability of criminal law norms and theories and the protection of civil liberties. In this respect, the focus of Chap. 2 is to demonstrate the theoretical premise for rationally responding to the gaps in the imputation for the negligence crime involving AI. Such premises not only exclude the possibility of AI as a subject of crime, but also establish the conceptual options for responding to crimes involving AI in the practice. All of these provide the premise for what follows in the in-depth argumentation and construction of the imputation system for the negligence crime involving AI.

Based on the conclusion argued in Chaps. 2 and 3, which is the focus of this study, aims to provide a rational imputation system for the negligence crime involving AI. To this end, the basic direction of theoretical efforts is to avoid the excessive reliance on the will factors in the imputation for the negligence crime, so as to achieve the transformation of imputation structure from will imputation to normative imputation. Accordingly, norms play a structural role in such criminal imputation, which not only reduces the overreliance on the subjective elements, such as will, in the imputation, but also broadens the scope of evaluation of criminal law norms. It is on this basis that some imputation elements such as behavior, result, and causality are transformed from the factual descriptions to the normative evaluations, which provides an ideal criminal imputation system to cope with the gaps in such imputation. However, how can this rational system of imputation be identified in the practical imputation for negligence crime involving AI? In this regard, this chapter provides an in-depth discussion on the three pillars, such as permitted risk, risk creation, and risk realization within the purpose scope of normative protection, so as to provide a reasonable imputation system for the negligence crime involving AI.

In contrast to the challenges that AI technology poses to the criminal imputation, it is perhaps much more urgent for us to think about how to reasonably address the risks and ethical concerns posed by such AI technology that is profoundly changing the direction of human social development without hindering its innovative development. As emphasized in the conclusion and future prospects in Chap. 4, the normative framework regulating AI technologies and their social impacts should be based on human consensus and common goals. Only when AI technology pays attention to human dignity and basic freedoms, adheres to cultural diversity and inclusiveness, and to basic ethics and morals, can AI technology develop in a responsible direction. In this context, dealing with the challenges brought about by the imputation for negligence crime involving AI is actually a matter of ethical concern for AI technology with the base of human dignity and freedom.

Beijing, China

Shuhong Zhao

Contents

Chapter 1
Challenge of Criminal Imputation for Negligence Crime Involving AI to the Traditional Criminal Imputation Theory

1.1 AI and Crime Involving AI

Academic research on the crime involving AI initially only focused on such crime that has already occurred and the strategies to deal with it. However, with the increasing penetration of AI applications in our daily life and the growing severity of AI-related crimes, academic research has focused much more on the criminal imputation for the crime involving AI. In this process, the presuppositional question facing scholars is what constitutes the crime involving AI?

Although people's efforts to unify the concept of AI may seem futile, this does not exclude the possibility to give a description of AI with the needs of legal research. Today, legal study on AI is still in its infancy, so the issues involved are mainly limited to the areas such as the legal status of AI, criminal liability and other topics. Therefore, most scholars choose representative AI technologies as research objects, such as autonomous driving technology, intelligent medical technology, etc. [1, 2] At this stage, the identified basic elements of the concept can be in fact sufficient to meet the needs of today's academic research. Of course, in addition to these basic elements, some vague elements in the concept of AI are still controversial. Some controversial issues, such as whether ATM machines and online shopping platform analysis software are AI technologies, do not in fact affect the conceptual basis of legal study on AI. Therefore, defining and understanding AI with the principal elements of the concept is by far the most reasonable choice.

1.1.1 Understanding AI with Its Characteristics

Broadly speaking, AI means teaching a machine how to do a task that was thought to be human [3]. AI has the ability, with which a digital computer or computer-controlled robot can perform tasks commonly associated with intelligent beings [4].

S. Zhao, *Principle of Criminal Imputation for Negligence Crime Involving Artificial Intelligence*, Artificial Intelligence and the Rule of Law,
https://doi.org/10.1007/978-981-97-0722-5_1

Although this concept is simple, it not only can meet the demands of academic research, but also can supply the understanding of the basic characteristics of AI. According to this concept, AI is characterized by five aspects [5, 6]. First, deep learning. Broadly, machine learning (ML) constitutes a foundational aspect of AI, concentrating on crafting algorithms that empower computers to acquire knowledge and formulate predictions or decisions through data analysis [7, 8]. Through this iterative process, ML model can improve its performance with each new dataset, eventually becoming more accurate and efficient [9]. Key concepts within Machine Learning are as following: supervised learning, unsupervised learning and reinforcement learning. Accordingly, deep learning is a subset of ML and employs artificial neural networks to simulate the hierarchical structure and function of the human brain. This approach enables the processing of vast amounts of data and the extraction of complex patterns or features.

For the deep learning, the applications are mainly in the following three areas: image recognition, natural language processing and generative adversarial networks. In the field of image recognition, deep learning techniques such as convolutional neural networks have revolutionized computer vision, enabling object detection, facial recognition, and image classification [10]. At the same time, with the natural language processing, techniques such as recurrent neural networks and transformers have significantly improved language understanding, translation, and generation. Finally, for the application of deep learning of AI, generative adversarial networks are capable of generating realistic images, videos, and other types of data by learning from existing datasets [11]. In terms of the application areas mentioned above, deep learning is able to transform raw data into the higher-level, more abstract expressions. Essentially, deep learning is about learning more useful features by building machine learning models with many hidden layers and massive amounts of training data to improve the accuracy of classification or prediction.

Second, cross-border integration. This aspect has two meanings, one of which refers to the fact that the emergence and development of AI technology is the result of the integration of multi-disciplinary knowledge, such as traditional mathematics and physics, as well as the emerging big data and supercomputing [12, 13]. Future trends will further promote the cross integration of AI with neuroscience, cognitive science, quantum science, psychology, economics, sociology and other related disciplines [14]. The other is that AI technology is widely used in various fields and integrated with the technical foundation of each field. For example, in emerging fields, AI is used in industries such as intelligent software and hardware, intelligent robots, intelligent delivery vehicles, virtual reality and augmented reality and intelligent terminals. Simply put, the cross-border integration of AI is reflected in the complexity of AI technology on the one hand, and the on the other hand, it is manifested in the wide range of applications of AI technology.

The third characteristics of AI is Human-in-the-Loop. Normally, most machine learning models rely on data that has been prepared by humans. However, the interaction between humans and machines does not stop there. In fact, the most powerful systems are set up such that they allow both sides to interact continuously through a mechanism commonly referred to as "Human in the Loop" [15, 16]. This practice of uniting human and machine intelligence creates a continuous feedback loop that allows the algorithm to produce better results each time. Human, as the service object, is at the center of the whole collaboration process, and his intention determines the response behavior of the AI. After decades of development, human-in-the-loop has been applied in many fields. For example, in the field of civil entertainment, based on hologram technology, virtual human–computer interaction is realized through wearable devices. In general, the harmonious relationship between human and AI has a number of benefits, including: ensuring accuracy, enhancing data collection, reducing bias and increasing efficiency [17, 18].

Openness to swarm-intelligence is the fourth basic characteristic of AI. According to the general understanding, swarm is a concept that explains how complicated social behavior can occur through easy, non-integrated individual actions. For instance, bee, ant, wasp or termite colonies show such self-united and mass intelligence [19]. Theoretically, swarm-intelligence is based on the collective behavior of elements in decentralized and self-organized systems [20]. In order to logically control the operations, swarm-intelligence has a great involvement in the field of Internet of Things (IoT) and IoT-based systems. As IoT-based systems are complex and consist of smart objects, so powerful decentralized algorithms supported by swarm-intelligence are used to resolve such complex problems. As important algorithm, swarm-intelligence algorithms are well established and applied in well-known aptitude-based problems where real-time actions are handled efficiently. In the field of artificial intelligence, the openness to swarm-intelligence means that individuals of AI are connected to the internet through the establishment of large databases, thus realizing real-time data sharing and transmission, and thereby supporting the effective realization of their intelligent functions.

As the last feature of artificial intelligence, autonomous control is the way AI controls and operates. It specifically includes three aspects of capabilities: autonomy, initiative, and responsiveness [21, 22]. In recent years, AI theories and methods represented by neural networks, fuzzy logic and evolutionary computing have been widely used in AI autonomous control, thus greatly improving the autonomous control capabilities of it. Autonomous control of AI means that it has satisfactory performance in the specific situations, where it is able to compensate for system failures without external intervention in the presence of significant uncertainty in the environment [23]. Compared with the control implemented in traditional mechanical automation, autonomous control of AI relatively relies on the construction of mathematical models of robots. Additionally, these control methods are very sensitive to the following situations, such as lack of sensor information, unplanned events, and unfamiliar locations in the robot operating environment. Therefore, traditional model-based machine automation cannot guarantee the stability of the designed system in complex environments, as well as the dynamic performance of the whole system [24].

In simple words, AI is the ability of machine to perform the cognitive functions we usually associate with human minds. As an effective tool, AI enables machines to learn from their experience, adapt to new changes and perform tasks just like humans.

1.1.2 Crime Involving AI

In recent years, technologies based on AI have achieved significant improvements in capability, accessibility and widespread deployment. From route-finding to language translation, biometric identification to political campaigning, and industrial process management to food supply logistics, AI permeates the modern connected world on many levels [25]. As AI technology expands in capability and deployment, the risk of criminal exploitation increases. Opportunities for crimes involving AI exist both in specific areas of computing and in the wider world. Some of these threats are extensions of existing criminal activity, while others may be new [26]. Therefore, there have been a number of recent efforts to identify and classify potential threats from the crimes involving AI [26–28]. The key question here is, how to understand crimes involving AI? And what are its basic types?

Thomas et al. [29] argues that evidence of crimes involving AI is provided by two research experiments. In the first one, two computational social scientists used AI as an instrument to convince social media users to click on phishing links within mass-produced messages. In this case, if some potential victim had clicked on the phishing link and filled in the subsequent web-form, then a criminal would have obtained personal and private information that could be used for theft and fraud. In the second research experiment, three computer scientists simulated a market and found that trading agents could learn and execute a "profitable" market manipulation campaign comprising a set of deceitful false-orders [30]. These two experiments show that AI provides a feasible and fundamentally novel threat, in the crimes involving AI.

Generally speaking, there are three main forms of crime involving AI, namely: crimes committed against AI; crimes committed by using AI and crimes caused by AI failing to fulfill the obligations to produce and manage safely [31–33]. Narrowly defined crimes involving AI include only the latter two categories, the former being intentional crimes and the latter being negligent crimes. The details are analyzed as following.

The first is the crime committed against AI. In the practice, the development and application of AI technology relies on the collection and use of a large amount of high-quality data and even a large amount of sensitive data. The collection and application of such data increases the risk of the protection of data and information by criminal law, as data and information not only possess strong political and economic value, but also relate to the personal privacy of citizens. Once the collected data information is leaked, it will bring serious harm to citizens, society and the state [12, 34, 35]. Additionally, AI has been widely used today in transportation, medical care, finance and other fields closely related to citizens' personal and property safety [36, 37]. In such fields, using AI as the target of crime will indirectly threaten the important rights and interests of citizens [26, 38]. For example, launching hacker attacks on the operating systems of self-driving cars will cause malfunctions of the self-driving systems and cause the traffic accidents, thus jeopardizing the rights and interests of our citizens' lives, health and property [39–41]. However, this type of crime is not the main category of crimes involving AI.

The second type of crime involving AI is in fact the use of AI as a criminal tool to commit the corresponding crime, and this type of act is an intentional crime. Today, with the widespread application of AI in our daily life, there are also various ways in which AI can be used illegally in a certain sense, and the possible scenarios in which AI is utilized as a tool for crime cover basically all traditional types of crim. For example, AI can be used to commit crimes endangering national security or national defense interests. Nowadays, data has become a national strategic resource, which has a bearing on national defense and international security. AI based on massive data can be used to steal, secretly gather, purchase, or illegally provide state secrets or intelligence for organization, institution, or personnel outside the country, thereby endangering national security. In addition, AI technology is widely used in military applications around the world today. The military application of AI technology can improve the accuracy of military strikes, expand the scope of destruction of military forces, and reduce direct human participation in the battlefield [42, 43]. This is also an unprecedented challenge to national security and national defense security.

AI can also be used to commit crimes that endanger public safety. In the practice, AI can be used to arson, breach dikes, cause explosions, spread pathogen of infectious diseases, poisonous or radioactive substances or other substances, or use other dangerous means to endanger public security. Additionally, as the combination of AI and the Internet further expands the openness of cyberspace, lower network access standards and conditions can easily be used by domestic and foreign terrorist and extremist forces to promote terrorism, extremism, and incitement to take terrorist attack, etc. [44]. In the field of autonomous driving, the participation of autonomous vehicles in the road traffic has also caused many traffic accidents, which indeed adds new safety risks to the public safety [45].

In the market economy, AI is increasingly used to commit crimes that undermine the market economic order and social management order. In the securities market, perpetrators can use AI technology to conduct in-depth learning and analysis of data to quickly grasp favorable information, or use the rapid response of AI robots to conduct high-frequency transactions, thereby plundering market wealth with extremely low risks [46–48]. In addition to the above-mentioned types of crimes, AI can be used to commit crimes of infringing upon the rights of the person and encroaching on property of it. Since AI possesses the characteristic of autonomous manipulation, it can relatively independently carry out crimes that infringe on the rights of person's life and health under the remote control of natural persons. In 2015, the 22-year-old worker at a Volkswagen production plant was "crushed to death" by a robotic arm. The worker was inside the "safety cage", meant to separate humans from the machines, to install a piece of the robot when an arm struck him, pinning him to a metal plate. He was resuscitated, and finally he died later at the hospital [49].

The third category of crimes involving AI is the crimes in which the person concerned fails to fulfill his duty of safety and management of the AI. Evidently, this kind of crime is a typical negligence crime and the actors of this kind of crimes include AI designers, producers, users [50]. Specifically, the above three types of actors have caused the occurrence of corresponding harmful results in the process of research, production and use due to their failure to fulfill their relevant obligations [51]. For example, designers of industrial AI did not comply with the requirements of the corresponding safety protection rules for large machinery and equipment during the research and development process, and ignored program settings such as mandatory stops that could protect the personal safety of workers in emergencies, resulting in serious consequences. Intelligent designers may need to bear the corresponding responsibility for the negligence in this regard [52–54].

In addition, if the manufacturer of AI fails to comply with the corresponding guidelines of occupational safety and health management system in the production process, or fails to recall the defective products in accordance with relevant requirements after the defective products enter the market, thus causing harmful consequences, the manufacturer will also need to bear the corresponding criminal responsibility [55, 56]. For another example, if a user of autonomous vehicle violates safety practice, such as regular maintenance, thereby causing a major traffic accident, the driver may be required to take corresponding responsibility for the negligent crime [57, 58].

From the above analysis of the types of crime involving AI, it can be found that this type of crime is mainly the crimes committed by using AI and the crimes caused by AI failing to fulfill its obligations to produce and manage safely. The first of these two crimes are intentional, while the second is negligent. With the perspective of criminal imputation, this study mainly focuses on the criminal imputation for these two types of crime involving AI.

1.1.3 Principal Characteristics of Crime Involving AI

Compared with the traditional crimes, what are the characteristics of crimes involving AI? In fact, the characteristics of them are the epitome of the impact of AI technology being used in illegal or criminal activities [59, 60]. Therefore, describing the characteristics of such crimes is an inevitable requirement for a comprehensive understanding of crimes involving artificial intelligence. In this regard, most views believe that the characteristics of crimes involving artificial intelligence depend on the characteristics of artificial intelligence—“deep learning, cross-border integration, human-in-the-loop, openness to swarm-intelligence and autonomous control” [31, 61, 62]. Therefore, this type of crime can be characterized in the following four aspects.

First, the subject of the crime is uncertain. Unlike the traditional “automation”, which aims to let machines simply and mechanically replace humans to complete some work, the “intelligence” of AI pursues the purpose of “human-in-the-loop” and emphasizes the ability of machines to more comprehensively and autonomously cooperate with people's work, so that AI can participate in the whole process of decision-making and execution [63, 64]. For example, smart healthcare uses a new generation of information technologies, such as big data, cloud computing, and AI, to transform the traditional medical system in an all-round way, making healthcare more efficient, more convenient, and more personalized [65]. In this process, intelligent robots also undertake the tasks of disease analysis, identification and treatment. In the case of humans using AI to commit crimes, the perpetrator and the AI also cooperate with each other, and thus man and machine work together to commit crimes, so that the two jointly dominate the results of the crime.

In addition, in crimes involving AI, if the perpetrator commits a crime because he fails to fulfill his obligations in safe production and management of AI, the relevant persons involved in the whole process from the design, production to use of AI may become the perpetrator of the crime [33, 66, 67]. It can be seen that the diversity and extensiveness of the participants in the crimes involving AI have led to the blurring and confusion of the criminal subjects.

Second, the complexity of the actus reus. With the development of AI technology, the new generation of AI is capable of deep learning. As we all know, deep learning is an algorithm that quickly trains deep neural networks, thereby giving AI the ability to learn independently and share information at its work, and use it to make decisions or guide its own work. This ability not only greatly improves the efficiency and accuracy of AI, but also eliminates the need for tedious programming [68–70]. When the perpetrator uses AI to commit a crime, the AI and the behavior of perpetrator are intertwined, thus jointly contributing to the outcome of the crime. Moreover, AI can make decisions independently, and its activities are highly professional and technical, which determines the complexity of criminal and harmful behaviors involving AI.

Finally, the perpetrators in the practice can operate remotely through AI technology and can even use encryption to hide their identities, which makes such crimes more covert [71–73]. For example, the criminals can use artificial intelligence technology to carry out cyberattacks without being personally involved. In addition, perpetrators can refine and intelligently design criminal acts through complex algorithms and procedures, which further enhances the covert nature of such crimes [74, 75].

Third, the complexity of the causality. Causation refers to the cause and effect of the event or action of a crime, and the result causing harm or damage, and is the capacity of one variable to influence another one. In the case of criminal law, if the first variable is of the fault of the cause, then he or she may be found guilty [76, 77]. With the deep learning, AI has the ability of autonomous manipulation. In practice, humans use AI to complete their work, and AI necessarily has an effect on the outcome of the work. When AI is used to commit crimes, the perpetrator and AI often work in tandem. As discussed before, AI can control autonomously in its work, so its role is often active in causing the results to occur. When the criminal result occurs, it is not easy to determine whether it is caused by the behavior of the perpetrator or driven by the participation of AI [78–80]. Between the perpetrator and AI, how to reasonably distribute the forces between the two that cause the result to occur is even more complicated.

For example, a doctor operated on a patient with the aid of a medical robot and caused the patient's death. In this case, the outcome of the patient's death could have been caused either by a procedural malfunction of the medical robot, or by the doctor's mishandling of the operation, or a combination of both. The core question here is, how to determine the contribution of medical robots and doctors' behavior in causing this result? In addition, when the designers, producers and users of AI fail to fulfill their obligations of safe production and management and then constitute a crime, it is more difficult to decide the causal relationship between the results of the crime and the violation of the obligations by different obligated subjects [50, 81].

Forth, the serious criminal consequences. Criminal consequences here refer to the damaging results of criminal behavior on society and individuals. With the widespread application of AI, the criminal consequences brought by it are often serious. As we all know, in the field of AI, openness to swarm-intelligence has become an important support for AI technology. Currently, AI has been connected to internet technology and big data technology, thus opening up the channels of access to swarm-intelligence and realizing the openness to swarm-intelligence. The realization of the openness to swarm-intelligence also makes crime more intelligent, leading to a further increase in the degree of harm caused by the results of crime [82, 83]. For example, by using fake audio and video to impersonate another person, the AI technology can cause various types of harms. The threats range from discrediting public figures to influence public opinion, to extorting funds by impersonating someone's child or relatives over a video call [84–86].

There are already examples of fake content undermining democracy in some countries: in the UK, for example, UK organization Future Advocacy used AI to create a fake video during the 2019 general election, which showed Boris Johnson and Jeremy Corbyn endorsing each other for prime minister. Although the video was not malicious, it stressed the potential of deepfakes to impact national politics. Additionally, with autonomous cars just around the corner, driverless vehicles were identified as a realistic delivery mechanism for explosives, or even as weapons of terror in their own right. As the number of AI systems multiplies in the critical areas such as public safety or financial transactions, the disruption of such AI-controlled systems for criminal or terrorist motives could result in widespread power failures, breakdown of food logistics, and overall country-wide chaos [87, 88].

Therefore, whether it is a crime committed by using AI or a crime caused by failing to fulfill the obligation of safe production and management of AI, the implementation of these crimes can easily cause unimaginable impacts and consequences.

1.2 Criminal Imputation Gaps for the Negligence Crime Involving AI

As an important norm for protecting legal interests, criminal law must respond with penalties to crimes involving AI that seriously infringe on citizens' rights and disrupt social order. However, when there stands a gap between criminal law norms and crimes involving AI, the criminal law is faced with the dilemma of how to apply to such crimes [89, 90]. In criminal law theory and judicial practice, this dilemma is mainly manifested in the difficulty of appropriately imputation for the crimes involving AI. Therefore, an in-depth analysis of the causes and effects of the attribution dilemma in AI-related crimes is the starting point for research on the criminal imputation for such crimes.

Generally speaking, to impute means to ascribe or attribute. In the criminal law theory, to impute is the action of attributing a person with knowledge, liability, duty, or other various forms of responsibility [91–93]. However, as mentioned before, in the field of crimes involving AI, traditional criminal imputation theory encounters a dilemma. The dilemma is that when the criminal law fails to comprehensively regulate the crimes involving AI, some of the criminal liability cannot be attributed to the appropriate subject of criminal liability. Essentially, this dilemma is how to reasonably allocate criminal liability among the criminal subjects [50, 80, 94]. This dilemma has resulted in some subjects who should have been criminally liable avoiding criminal liability, or imposing some criminal liability on subjects who need not be criminally liable. It can be seen that there stands a criminal imputation gap in the field of criminal imputation for crimes involving AI [95, 96]. This gap is the imputation dilemma caused by AI technology in the field of criminal law.

However, does this criminal imputation gap exist in all the crimes involving AI? In essence, just as what we have discussed before, these crimes involved mainly fall into two categories, namely, crimes using AI and crimes involving failure to fulfill production and management obligations for AI. The former is an intentional crime, while the latter is a negligent crime. Therefore, this part focuses on the criminal imputation gap for these two types of crimes involving AI.

1.2.1 Imputation Gap in the Intentional Crime Involving AI

As far as the current development level of artificial intelligence is concerned, AI have not had the ability to recognize and control independently that some researchers claim [67, 80]. Of course, the ability of AI to self-learning and self-development are properties that allow this new formation to compete with the human intelligence and perform actions that put it on a par with humans. However, AI is not yet in the practice capable to act autonomously like a person without being separated from the scope of the program prepared by the developer or programmer. Therefore, the current intentional crimes involving AI does not mean that the AI commits a crime intentionally, but rather that a person as the perpetrator utilizes AI to intentionally commit a crime, in which AI is merely a tool for committing a crime [97, 98].

When a person uses AI to commit a crime, he still undoubtedly remains liable for the results of the crime caused by the AI if the AI accurately carries out the perpetrator's instructions. However, AI, after all, is different from the traditional criminal tools. The functional characteristics of AI such as deep learning and autonomous control have caused the subjects of the intentional crimes involving AI to be ambiguous, actus reus, and causal relationships to be extremely complicated. These facts affect the perpetrator's ability to control his own behavior, which may lead to the combat error in criminal law [99, 100].

Specifically, because AI has the technology, such as deep learning, cross-border integration, autonomous manipulation and other technologies, these technologies give AI the ability to collect data to guide its own activities to a certain extent. In this process, the actor's control over the AI is relatively weakened, which also implies a relative weakening of the actor's ability to control his own behavior [67, 101]. In this case, if the perpetrator does not impose any coercive intervention on the AI, the perpetrator will not be able to dominate the activities of the AI in a relatively effective manner [50, 99]. Once the AI is detached from the perpetrator's instructions, the activities it performs during the commission of the crime will deviate from the perpetrator's intentions, so the question that arises is: how to reasonably evaluate the criminal responsibility of the perpetrator? Indeed, this relates to the theory of mistake of fact in the criminal law, including concrete and abstract mistake of fact. Mistakes of fact arise when the perpetrator misunderstood some fact that negates an element of the crime. Therefore, this can be discussed from the following two aspects.

Firstly, the concrete mistake of fact. The kind of mistake of fact means that the fact recognized by the perpetrator does not coincide with the fact that actually occurred. However, it is not outside the scope of the constitution of the crime, i.e., the perpetrator has only made a mistake in recognizing the fact within the scope of a certain criminal element [102]. For example, perpetrator A wants to use an AI robot to murder B, but the robot kills C in the course of specifically carrying out the perpetrator's instructions. In this case, due to the AI robot, the perpetrator's behavioral deviation caused the perpetrator's intended murderer to be inconsistent with the actual victim, but this inconsistency did not exceed the scope of the criminal elements of murder. In the criminal theory, there are two main views on how to deal with the perpetrator's criminal responsibility for this kind of mistake: The first is the specific conformity theory, which holds that since the result of the crime does not specifically conform to the subjective intent of the perpetrator, the perpetrator is liable for attempting the crime he intended to commit, but he is liable for negligence in respect of the crime embodied in the result of the crime. However, since there is only one act, imaginary conflict is established and punished as a felony. According to the specific conformity theory, the perpetrator A in this case is liable to B for the attempted intentional homicide and to C for causing death by negligence. Since these two criminal acts are imaginary conflicts, A should bear criminal responsibility for the attempted homicide in accordance with the principle of punishment from a felony.

The second is the legal conformity theory, which holds that the perpetrator should bear the criminal responsibility for the accomplished crime he intended to commit. In this case, the perpetrator in fact committed the act of murder and caused the death of the victim [103, 104]. Although the criminal object that the offender intended to infringe was inconsistent with the actual victim, there is no difference in the meaning of the criminal law protection of the right to life, since both are equally protected by the constituent elements of the crime of murder. According to the legal conformity theory, A's behavior in the case fully meets all the constituent elements of the crime of murder, and therefore A should bear criminal liability for homicide. Compared with the specific conformity theory, the legal conformity theory is the common view in the criminal law theory and judicial practice today [105].

Secondly, the abstract mistake of fact. This kind of mistake refer to the facts recognized by the perpetrator and the facts that occurred in reality, which respectively belong to the different specific constitutions of the crime. For example, perpetrator A wants to use an intelligent robot to kill B. However, the intelligent robot does not kill B during the specific execution, but damages C's valuable vase. In this case, the perpetrator used AI to commit the crime, but the perpetrator's actions were deviated due to the AI. As a result, there was an inconsistency between the object that the perpetrator intended to victimize and the object that was actually victimized, and this inconsistency went beyond the constitutive elements of the identified crime. There are likewise two views on how to deal with such abstract mistake of fact in the criminal law theory: one is the abstract conformity theory. According to this view, to the extent that the constitutive facts known to the perpetrator are consistent with the constitutive facts that actually occurred, the actor's behavior constitutes the consummation of an intentional crime [106, 107], the other is the statutory conformity theory. This theory holds that the mistakes between different criminal constitutions cannot in principle constitute an intentional crime or only constitute the criminal attempt. Even if the criminal constitutive elements are different, if the crimes are homogeneous, then consummation of an intentional crime is established within the limits of overlap.

In the second case, the crime that perpetrator A wanted to commit was homicide, but what actually happened was intentional destruction of public or private property. Essentially, homicide belongs to the category of crimes against the personal rights of citizens, while the crime of intentional destruction of property belongs to the crimes against property, and these two crimes are therefore not qualitatively the same. In addition, subjective culpability of the perpetrator for damaging property is only negligence rather than intentionality, and most countries do not stipulate that negligent destruction of property is a crime. Therefore, the perpetrator A in this case constitutes attempted intentional homicide. With regards to the abstract mistake of fact, judicial practice generally deals with them in accordance with the following two situations [108, 109]. First, the perpetrator originally intended to commit a felony, but objectively what he committed was a misdemeanor crime. In this case, the offender constitutes an attempted felony; secondly, the perpetrator intended to commit a misdemeanor, but objectively it was a felony. In this case, the offender constitutes a completed misdemeanor [110, 111].

In addition to the two kinds of mistakes of fact mentioned above, the use of AI in the commission of the crime also reduces the perpetrator's ability to control himself. In this case, does the perpetrator not bear criminal liability or only bear reduced criminal liability? In this regard, according to the theory of actio libera in causa, we can give a negative answer to this question. As a law principle, actio libera in causa means that even if the person was not free to choose the course of action while performing an offence, he can still be held responsible for it if he voluntarily created a condition for the offending action [112, 113]. According to the theory of action libera in causa, when the perpetrator is aware of the relevant intelligent attributes of the AI, he still uses it to commit the crime. Although the perpetrator's control ability is diminished due to the AI activities, when it commits a crime other than that was intended by the perpetrator, he still needs to bear criminal responsibility for the consequences of the above crime, and the provisions on mitigating or alleviating the punishment cannot be applied.

From the above discussion, it can be found that AI as a criminal tool does bring different changes to the implementation of intentional crimes, such as the emergence of deviations between criminal behavior and criminal results, as well as the weakening of the perpetrator's ability to control. However, these changes have been addressed by corresponding theories in traditional criminal law theories. Although there are still some disputes in theory, relevant discussions have provided reasonable solutions to solve the problem. Even if, according to some scholars, AI develops to the point where it has full cognitive and control capabilities, it is still possible to attribute responsibility to the perpetrator through the theory of indirect perpetration in the field of intentional crimes. Therefore, in cases where AI is utilized to commit intentional crimes, the existing criminal law theory is sufficient to cope with the predictable changes brought about by AI without the dilemma of attribution that leads to the imputation gaps.

In short, the problem of criminal imputation for crimes involving AI mainly deals with negligence crimes rather than intentional crimes. Therefore, the focus of this study is mainly on the study of the imputation for the negligent crimes involving AI.

1.2.2 Imputation Gap in the Negligence Crimes Involving AI

According to the previous discussion, crimes involving AI are mainly the negligent crimes, i.e., crimes in which the perpetrator fails to fulfill his obligation of safe production as well as the obligation of management of AI. In theory and practice, the difficulties in criminal imputation for the negligent crimes involving AI are mainly reflected in the following two aspects; first, AI products with a certain degree of autonomy contribute to the occurrence of criminal results to a certain extent. In this case, is it necessary to take into account the AI product with a certain degree of autonomy in the allocation of criminal imputation? Secondly, with the involvement of AI in the commission of crimes, the judgment of the perpetrator's possibility of foresight as well as the possibility of avoidance is very different from the traditional theories, and therefore the criminal imputation for the negligent crime has a high degree of uncertainty.

Generally speaking, criminal negligence refers to a defendant who acts in disregard of a serious risk of harm that a reasonable person in the same situation would have perceived. Accordingly, criminal imputation for the negligent crimes is usually based on the possibility of foreseeing from the perpetrator and the causation. At the same time, the empirical facts are used as the standard of judgment for specific issues in the criminal imputation [114, 115]. According to the previous discussion of the characteristics of crimes involving AI, such crimes will have a series of impacts on the theory and structure of imputation for the negligence crimes, and these impacts are the important reasons for the formation of the imputation gap of the crimes involving AI. Specifically, this can be illustrated in the following aspects.

Firstly, AI technology can cause offenders to fail to foresee the consequences of their behaviors. The possibility to foresee the result from the perpetrator is the basis of imputation for the crime of negligence. If the perpetrator does not have the possibility to foresee the occurrence of the harmful result, he cannot be held responsible for the harmful result. For example, navigation products used for road transportation are now commonly characterized by intelligent attributes. Such products can obtain big data such as traffic and weather by connecting to the Internet, so that they can update the planning and selection of roads in real time. In this case, the intelligent system uses the conclusions of its deep learning to guide the choice of the driving path. Therefore, the designers and producers of the intelligent navigation product cannot in fact foresee the possibility of intelligent activities of the intelligent navigation system outside the scope of its programming [116–118].

There is no doubt that the realization of autonomy of AI to a certain extent has weakened the possibility of the its designers, producers, users and other related personnel to foresee the consequences of their actions. In particular, with the continuous development of AI technology, the fact that AI products obtain data information and act accordingly likewise reduces the ability to foresee the actions of the related persons. For example, autonomous driving technology has achieved the operational functions based on awareness, decision-making, and action. In detail, the autonomous driving system receives real-time data information about the traffic environment, such as vehicles, pedestrians, traffic signals, and traffic signs, and then makes decisions such as turning, slowing down, and stopping [119, 120]. With the complex and changeable traffic environment and the autonomous adaptability of autonomous driving technology, the autonomy of autonomous driving technology also creates obstacles for drivers to judge the possibility of foreseeing.

Although humans have designed, built and deployed them, their behavior is not subject to direct human instructions, but rather is a response to the results of the analysis and judgment of the information available to them [121, 122]. Their reactions and decisions in different contexts are likewise not something that their programmers, makers, and other relevant people might anticipate or control in advance. Nowadays, in a society where AI is increasingly integrated into people's daily lives, the extensive use of intelligent machines and intelligent systems is continuously reducing people's awareness and prediction of their own behavior. This will undoubtedly pose various challenges to the basis and construction of criminal imputation for the negligent crimes involving AI.

Secondly, the application of AI technology makes causality complex and complicated, thus posing the challenges to the reasonable distribution of criminal liability. For the negligent crimes, the occurrence of harmful results is one of the necessary elements for attribution of liability. Therefore, there must stand a causal relationship between the criminal outcome and the harmful behavior [123, 124]. If it cannot be determined that there is such causality, then it cannot be certain that the result was caused by the behavior, and thus the criminal liability for the negligent crime cannot be attributed to the corresponding subject [125]. In the field of traditional negligence crimes, such causality can generally be determined clearly and certainly. For example, due to the negligence of the designer of the navigation product, he did not incorporate the corresponding response mechanism for bad weather into the navigation program, causing the driver to fall into the river and died when driving his vehicle according to the navigation in the dense fog. In this case, the development of the whole causal process is in line with the development principle of things and the judgment of human experience, so the causality can be clearly determined.

However, in case of crimes involving AI, due to the characteristics of AI such as deep learning, coupled with the inherent complexity of AI technology and applications, determining the causal process of crimes involving AI is in fact beyond the ability of the average person [90, 126]. For example, intelligent navigation product generally has the ability to automatically acquire data in an open network for its deep learning. Therefore, in its application, it is difficult for person to find out afterward what kind of calculations were made and what kind of data filtering criteria were adopted. In the process of autonomous manipulation of AI, a black hole of data and a dark box of operation have been formed objectively [127, 128]. Throughout the causal process, the autonomous activity of AI almost blurs a certain stage in the course of the events, which makes the causal process interrupted because it cannot be ascertained. Consequently, because the causal relationship between behavior and results is difficult or even impossible to identify, this poses a challenge to the imputation for the negligent crimes involving AI.

Thirdly, the lack of pre-existing norms related to AI technology poses a challenge to the judgment care duty in the negligence crimes. Normally, the negligent crime occurs when one should foresee that his act may cause socially dangerous consequences but fails to do so because of carelessness or, having foreseen the consequences, readily assumes he can prevent them, with the result that these consequences occur. In such crime, the actor violates two duties, namely the duty to foresee the consequences and the duty to avoid the consequences [129, 130]. Therefore, these two obligations are the key to determining whether the perpetrator committed a crime of negligence. Today, in the fields such as transportation and industrial production, which are inherently characterized by a certain degree of risk, there are various operating regulations and rules designed to ensure the life safety and social order. If the actor violates these rules and causes corresponding consequences, the actor needs to bear responsibility for his violation of his duty to foresee and avoid this consequence.

For the traditional negligence crimes, since the criminal acts and the scenarios involved are relatively usual, the obligation to foresee and avoid the results of the perpetrator can be judged on the basis of legal obligations, statutory obligations, professional requirements and entrusted obligations. However, in the negligent crimes involving AI, the challenge is how to determine such duties. Generally speaking, there are at least three types of such duties in the field of AI: the first is the duty to ensure the safe regulation and prudent research and development of the technology; the second is the duty to promptly eliminate the hidden dangers in the manufacture and sale of the product, and the third is the duty to comply with the requirements of the standards for the normal use of the AI products [131–133]. However, in practice, the unified technical standards and industry guidelines for AI research and development do not exist, and the regulations and laws related to AI products have likewise not been established. However, in practice, unified technical standards and industry guidelines for AI research and development do not exist, and regulatory laws and regulations related to AI products have likewise not been established. Therefore, although the direction of the source of such duties can be clarified, the delineation of the specific duty of care is still unattainable.

The standards for the use of AI products specifically include the following requirements: procedural obligations for the operation of the product such as input, clicking, and management, obligations for the security of the information origin in the process of data aggregation, and the obligations for the maintenance of the algorithmic system in the process of its operation, and so on [134, 135]. However, because these obligations lack the relevant regulations and laws, industry standards, common sense, etc., this undoubtedly increases the difficulty in identifying the corresponding duties of the actors. For the negligent crimes, such difficulty in identifying the care duty of the perpetrator poses a challenge to the imputation for the negligent crime involving AI.

Fourthly, the development and application of AI technology has brought the challenge to the traditional imputation structure of the negligence crimes. Criminal law theory generally holds that negligent criminals have no possibility to commit the joint crime [136–138]. For the traditional negligence crimes, this imputation structure will not have a major negative impact on the attribution of criminal liability. In the traditional agricultural or industrial societies, human beings are largely able to dominate part or all of the developmental process of an event. Even when this process required some collaboration between people, the division of labor among individuals was relatively identified and simple, and their roles were reasonably well differentiated. In this context, individuals are able to assume their own, clearly bounded responsibility for the harmful consequences of their actions. For example, for a certain product, according to the traditional theory of imputation, the designer of it bears the responsibility related to his own act of design, while the producer bears the responsibility related to his own act of production. Although their behavior is in the production process of this product, they have relatively independent work duties and areas of responsibility [139, 140].

However, the crimes involving AI pose a challenge to the application of this traditional imputation theory. As we all know, the outcome of AI products cannot be separated from the contribution of the swarm-intelligence and cross-border integration [141, 142]. Objectively, the research and development, production and application of AI products require the participation of a large number of people, and this cannot be accomplished by a certain person or group of people alone. For example, AI cannot have deep learning capabilities without big data. As we all know, such big data widely originates from the internet users, and the data generated by these users in their production and life forms a data pool that is sufficient to support AI for its deep learning. Moreover, the research and development of AI technology requires knowledge and technology from many disciplines, such as internet, computers, brain science, bionics etc. Therefore, in the design and production of AI products, the traditional production module and technology partition have been broken, and it is difficult for designers and producers to identify their duties. Therefore, the imputation for the negligence crimes involving AI has to consider the connection of duties between actors and the distribution of the duty scope assumed between different actors.

From the above analysis, it can be found that there stand many imputation gaps in the criminal imputation for the negligent crimes involving AI due to the characteristics of such crimes. In criminal imputation for crimes involving AI, such imputation gaps undoubtedly pose theoretical and practical challenges to the traditional imputation theory for the negligent crime. These challenges are mainly reflected in the inability to reasonably allocate liability for the different participants in this type of crime.

In the negligent crimes involving AI, it is almost impossible for the perpetrator to foresee the specific result and the basic part of the causal process, which limits the scopes for the application of the traditional imputation for the negligent crime. It is well known that the criminal imputation for the traditional negligent crimes is based on the perpetrator's duty to foresee the result as well as the duty to avoid the result [143, 144]. This can normally lead to two unreasonable results of imputation for the negligent crime in the judicial practice: first, regarding the foreseeability, the risk inherent in the AI technology itself is directly used to infer the perpetrator's foresight of the danger of the behavior, thereby expanding the scope of the crime of negligence; second, the particularity of AI technology is used to deny the possibility of foreseeability by the perpetrator, thereby unreasonably narrowing the scope of criminal imputation for the negligent crime involving AI. The reason for this dilemma lies in whether it is a concrete or abstract danger that the perpetrator of a negligent crime is required to foresee with respect to the result as well as the causal relationship.

In short, as the crimes involving AI have owned the characteristics that are different from those of the traditional crimes, the traditional theories have encountered unprecedented challenges in imputation for such crimes. This challenge manifests itself primarily in the gap created by the criminal imputation for the negligent crime involving AI. This criminal imputation gap may cause the perpetrator that should bear criminal responsibility to escape his responsibility, while the perpetrator that do not need to bear criminal responsibility bears certain responsibility. This imputation gap has no possibility to arise in the intentional crimes committed using AI. In this type of crime, because the attributes of the AI product as a criminal tool have not changed, the mistake theory in the criminal law can completely achieve the reasonable imputation for the crimes. Moreover, in the particular circumstances of such intentional crime, criminal imputation may reasonably be made with the criminal theory of indirect principal offender.

Accordingly, the imputation gap for crimes involving AI is mainly found in the negligent crimes. This kind of crime is a negligence crime in which the perpetrator fails to fulfill his obligation of safe production and management of AI products. The traditional imputation for such crime is based on the perpetrator's obligation to foresee or avoid the result. However, such crime is different from the traditional negligent crime and these differences have posed a theoretical challenge to the traditional theory of imputation.

References

1. Cui G, Zhang W, Xiao Y, Yao L, Fang Z (2022) Cooperative perception technology of autonomous driving in the internet of vehicles environment: a review. Sensors 22(15):5535. https://doi.org/10.3390/s22155535
2. Imai T (2019) Legal regulation of autonomous driving technology: current conditions and issues in Japan. IATSS Res 43(2):263–267. https://doi.org/10.1016/j.iatssr.2019.11.009
3. Arruda A (2017) An ethical obligation to use artificial intelligence? An examination of the use of artificial intelligence in law and the model rules of professional responsibility. Am J Trial Adv 40(3):443–458
4. Du-Harpur X, Watt FM, Luscombe NM, Lynch MD (2020) What is AI? Applications of artificial intelligence to dermatology. Br J Dermatol 183(3):423–430. https://doi.org/10.1111/bjd.18880
5. Raschka S, Patterson J, Nolet C (2020) Machine learning in python: main developments and technology trends in data science, machine learning, and artificial intelligence. Information 11(4):193. https://doi.org/10.3390/info11040193
6. Wang A, Xiu X, Liu S, Qian Q, Wu S (2022) Characteristics of artificial intelligence clinical trials in the field of healthcare: a cross-sectional study on ClinicalTrials.gov. Int J Environ Res Public Health 19(20):13691
7. Helm JM, Swiergosz AM, Haeberle HS, Karnuta JM, Schaffer JL, Krebs VE et al (2020) Machine learning and artificial intelligence: definitions, applications, and future directions. Curr Rev Muscul Med 13:69–76. https://doi.org/10.1007/s12178-020-09600-8
8. Ma LY, Sun BH (2020) Machine learning and AI in marketing: Connecting computing power to human insights. Int J Res Market 37:481–504. https://doi.org/10.1016/j.ijresmar.2020.04.005
9. Ghillani D (2022) Deep learning and artificial intelligence framework to improve the cyber security. https://doi.org/10.22541/au.166379475.54266021/v1
10. Pak M, Kim S (2017) A review of deep learning in image recognition. In: Proceedings of the 2017 4th international conference on computer applications and information processing technology (CAIPT), Kuta Bali, pp 1–3. https://doi.org/10.1109/CAIPT.2017.8320684
11. Sohn K, Sung CE, Koo G, Kwon O (2021) Artificial intelligence in the fashion industry: consumer responses to generative adversarial network (GAN) technology. Int J Retail Distrib Manag 49(1):61–80. https://doi.org/10.1108/IJRDM-03-2020-0091
12. Jakka G, Yathiraju N, Ansari MF (2022) Artificial intelligence in terms of spotting malware and delivering cyber risk management. J Posit School Psychol 6(3):6156–6165
13. Qiu Y, Tang Z, Luo Y (2023) Cross-border technology integration in the field of artificial intelligence based on neural network algorithm. In: Li A, Shi Y, Xi L (eds) 6GN for future wireless networks. 6GN 2022. Lecture notes of the institute for computer sciences, social informatics and telecommunications engineering, vol 505. Springer, Cham. https://doi.org/10.1007/978-3-031-36014-5_7
14. Li Y (2022). Research on the practice of cross integration of "artificial intelligence + X" new engineering disciplines. In: Proceedings of the 11th international conference on educational and information technology (ICEIT), Chengdu, China, pp 246–251. https://doi.org/10.1109/ICEIT54416.2022.9690632
15. Mosqueira-Rey E, Hernández-Pereira E, Alonso-Ríos D, Bobes-Bascarán J, Fernández-Leal Á (2023) Human-in-the-loop machine learning: a state of the art. Artif Intell Rev 56(4):3005–3054. https://doi.org/10.1007/s10462-022-10246-w
16. Zanzotto FM (2019) Human-in-the-loop artificial intelligence. J Artif Intell Res 64:243–252. https://doi.org/10.1613/jair.1.11345
17. Berberich N, Nishida T, Suzuki S (2020) Harmonizing artificial intelligence for social good. Philos Technol 33:613–638. https://doi.org/10.1007/s13347-020-00421-8
18. Lu Y, Adrados JS, Chand SS, Wang L (2021) Humans are not machines—anthropocentric human–machine symbiosis for ultra-flexible smart manufacturing. Engineering 7(6):734–737. https://doi.org/10.1016/j.eng.2020.09.018

19. Martinez-Torres R, Olmedilla M (2016) Identification of innovation solvers in open innovation communities using swarm intelligence. Technol Forecast Soc Change 109:15–24. https://doi.org/10.1016/j.techfore.2016.05.007
20. Beni G (2020) Swarm intelligence. In: Sotomayor M, Pérez-Castrillo D, Castiglione F (eds) Complex social and behavioral systems. Encyclopedia of complexity and systems science series. Springer, New York. https://doi.org/10.1007/978-1-0716-0368-0_530
21. Aibin M, Aldiab M, Bhavsar R, Lodhra J, Reyes M, Rezaeian F et al (2021) Survey of RPAS autonomous control systems using artificial intelligence. IEEE Access 9:167580–167591. https://doi.org/10.1109/ACCESS.2021.3136226
22. Khayyam H, Javadi B, Jalili M, Jazar RN (2020) Artificial intelligence and internet of things for autonomous vehicles. In: Jazar R, Dai L (eds) Nonlinear approaches in engineering applications. Springer, Cham. https://doi.org/10.1007/978-3-030-18963-1_2
23. Chanda SS, Banerjee DN (2022) Omission and commission errors underlying AI failures. AI Soc 22:1–24. https://doi.org/10.1007/s00146-022-01585-x
24. Fragapane G, De Koster R, Sgarbossa F, Strandhagen JO (2021) Planning and control of autonomous mobile robots for intralogistics: literature review and research agenda. Eur J Oper Res 294(2):405–426. https://doi.org/10.1016/j.ejor.2021.01.019
25. Benaich N, Hogarth I (2019) State of AI report 2019. SlideShare. https://www.slideshare.net/StateofAIReport/state-of-ai-report-2019-151804430. Accessed 25 Jun 2019
26. Caldwell M, Andrews JT, Tanay T, Griffin LD (2020) AI-enabled future crime. Crime Sci 9(1):1–13. https://doi.org/10.1186/s40163-020-00123-8
27. Sivaram J, Narrain JM, Honnavalli P, Eswaran S (2023) Adversarial machine learning: the rise in AI-enabled crime. Comput Fraud Sec 2023(2):9
28. Wilner AS (2018) Cybersecurity and its discontents: artificial intelligence, the Internet of Things, and digital misinformation. Int J 73(2):308–316. https://doi.org/10.1177/0020702018782496
29. Thomas SL, Nafus D, Sherman J (2018) Algorithms as fetish: faith and possibility in algorithmic work. Big Data Soc 5(1). https://doi.org/10.1177/2053951717751552
30. Martínez-Miranda E, McBurney P, Howard MJ (2016) Learning unfair trading: A market manipulation analysis from the reinforcement learning perspective. In: Proceedings of the 2016 IEEE conference on evolving and adaptive intelligent systems, EAIS 2016, pp 103–109. https://doi.org/10.1109/EAIS.2016.7502499.
31. Begishev IR, Kirillov MA, Bersei DD, Nechaeva EV, Perepelkin VI, Serkova TV et al (2023) Robotics, artificial intelligence and criminal law: an overview of contemporary studies. In: AIP conference proceedings, vol 2701. AIP Publishing LLC, p 020033. https://doi.org/10.1063/5.0130210
32. Sukhodolov AP, Bychkov AV, Bychkova AM (2020) Criminal policy for crimes committed using artificial intelligence technologies: state, problems, prospects. https://doi.org/10.17516/1997-1370-0542
33. Yeoh P (2019) Artificial intelligence: accelerator or panacea for financial crime? J Finan Crime 26(2):634–646. https://doi.org/10.1108/JFC-08-2018-0077
34. Lee P, Bubeck S, Petro J (2023) Benefits, limits, and risks of GPT-4 as an AI chatbot for medicine. New Engl J Med 388(13):1233–1239. https://doi.org/10.1056/NEJMsr2214184
35. Song M, Xing X, Duan Y, Cohen J, Mou J (2022) Will artificial intelligence replace human customer service? The impact of communication quality and privacy risks on adoption intention. J Retail Consum Serv 66:102900. https://doi.org/10.1016/j.jretconser.2021.102900
36. Huang MH, Rust RT (2021) Engaged to a robot? The role of AI in service. J Serv Res 24(1):30–41. https://doi.org/10.1177/1094670520902266
37. Secinaro S, Calandra D, Secinaro A, Muthurangu V, Biancone P (2021) The role of artificial intelligence in healthcare: a structured literature review. BMC Med Inform Decis Mak 21:1–23. https://doi.org/10.1186/s12911-021-01488-9
38. Blauth TF, Gstrein OJ, Zwitter A (2022) Artificial intelligence crime: an overview of malicious use and abuse of AI. IEEE Access 10:77110–77122. https://doi.org/10.1109/ACCESS.2022.3191790

39. Grigorescu S, Trasnea B, Cocias T, Macesanu G (2020) A survey of deep learning techniques for autonomous driving. J Field Robot 37(3):362–386. https://doi.org/10.1002/rob.21918
40. Sestino A, Peluso AM, Amatulli C, Guido G (2022) Let me drive you! The effect of change seeking and behavioral control in the artificial intelligence-based self-driving cars. Technol Soc 70:102017. https://doi.org/10.1016/j.techsoc.2022.102017
41. Soldatov MA, Butova VV, Pashkov D, Butakova MA, Medvedev PV, Chernov AV, Soldatov AV (2021) Self-driving laboratories for development of new functional materials and optimizing known reactions. Nanomaterials 11(3):619. https://doi.org/10.3390/nano11030619
42. Davis Z (2019) Artificial intelligence on the battlefield. PRism 8(2):114–131
43. Kandybko N, Zemlina O, Plaksa V, Dmitriev A (2023) Application of artificial intelligence technologies in the context of military security and civil infrastructure protection. In: AIP conference proceedings, vol 2476. AIP Publishing. https://doi.org/10.1063/5.0103281
44. Ionescu B, Ghenescu M, Răstoceanu F, Roman R, Buric M (2020) Artificial intelligence fights crime and terrorism at a new level. IEEE Multimedia 27(2):55–61. https://doi.org/10.1109/MMUL.2020.2994403
45. Atakishiyev S, Salameh M, Yao H, Goebel R (2021) Explainable artificial intelligence for autonomous driving: a comprehensive overview and field guide for future research directions. arXiv preprint arXiv:2112.11561. https://doi.org/10.48550/arXiv.2112.11561
46. Harris H (2022) Artificial intelligence and policing of financial crime: a legal analysis of the state of the field. Finan Technol Law Combat Finan Crime 20:281–299. https://doi.org/10.1007/978-3-030-88036-1_12
47. Kurshan E, Shen H, Yu H (2020) Financial crime and fraud detection using graph computing: application considerations and outlook. In: Proceedings of the 2020 second international conference on transdisciplinary AI (TransAI). IEEE, pp 125–130. https://doi.org/10.1109/TransAI49837.2020.00029.
48. Sadaf R, McCullagh O, Sheehan B, Grey C, King E, Cunneen M (2021) Algorithmic trading, high-frequency trading: implications for MiFID II and market abuse regulation (MAR) in the EU. High-frequency trading: implications for MiFID II and market abuse regulation (MAR) in the EU. https://doi.org/10.2139/ssrn.3846814
49. Karthike T (2023) Automation, robotics and artificial intelligence: labourers' ally or enemy? Indian J Integ Res Law 3:1. https://doi.org/10.2139/ssrn.4330147
50. Osmani N (2020) The complexity of criminal liability of AI systems. Masaryk Univ J Law Technol 14(1):53–82. https://doi.org/10.5817/MUJLT2020-1-3
51. Madaio M, Egede L, Subramonyam H, Wortman Vaughan J, Wallach H (2022) Assessing the fairness of AI systems: AI practitioners' processes, challenges, and needs for support. In: Proceedings of the ACM on human–computer interaction, 6(CSCW1), pp 1–26. https://doi.org/10.1145/3512899
52. Bikeev I, Kabanov P, Begishev I, Khisamova Z (2019) Criminological risks and legal aspects of artificial intelligence implementation. In: Proceedings of the international conference on artificial intelligence, information processing and cloud computing, pp 1–7. https://doi.org/10.1145/3371425.3371476
53. Naik N, Hameed BM, Shetty DK, Swain D, Shah M, Paul R et al (2022) Legal and ethical consideration in artificial intelligence in healthcare: who takes responsibility? Front Surg 9:266. https://doi.org/10.3389/fsurg.2022.862322
54. Stahl BC (2023) Embedding responsibility in intelligent systems: from AI ethics to responsible AI ecosystems. Sci Rep 13(1):7586. https://doi.org/10.1038/s41598-023-34622-w
55. Chesterman S (2020) Artificial intelligence and the limits of legal personality. Int Comp Law Quart 69(4):819–844. https://doi.org/10.1017/S0020589320000366
56. Nyholm S (2023) Responsibility gaps, value alignment, and meaningful human control over artificial intelligence. In: Risk and responsibility in context. Routledge, pp 191–213. https://doi.org/10.4324/9781003276029-14
57. Hevelke A, Nida-Rümelin J (2015) Responsibility for crashes of autonomous vehicles: an ethical analysis. Sci Eng Ethics 21:619–630. https://doi.org/10.1007/s11948-014-9565-5

58. Zhai S, Wang L, Liu P (2023) Human and machine drivers: sharing control, sharing responsibility. Accid Anal Prevent 188:107096. https://doi.org/10.1016/j.aap.2023.107096
59. Dilek S, Çakır H, Aydın M (2015) Applications of artificial intelligence techniques to combating cyber crimes: a review. arXiv preprint arXiv:1502.03552. https://doi.org/10.48550/arXiv.1502.03552
60. Hayward KJ, Maas MM (2021) Artificial intelligence and crime: a primer for criminologists. Crime Media Cult 17(2):209–233. https://doi.org/10.1177/1741659020917434
61. Ali A, Syed AM (2020) Cyberbullying detection using machine learning. Pak J Eng Technol 3(2):45–50
62. Hosny A, Parmar C, Quackenbush J, Schwartz LH, Aerts HJ (2018) Artificial intelligence in radiology. Nat Rev Cancer 18(8):500–510. https://doi.org/10.1038/s41568-018-0016-5
63. Cimini C, Pirola F, Pinto R, Cavalieri S (2020) A human-in-the-loop manufacturing control architecture for the next generation of production systems. J Manuf Syst 54:258–271. https://doi.org/10.1016/j.jmsy.2020.01.002
64. Samad T (2023) Human-in-the-loop control and cyber–physical–human systems: applications and categorization. In: Cyber–physical–human systems: fundamentals and applications, pp 1–23. https://doi.org/10.1002/9781119857433.ch1
65. Tian S, Yang W, Le Grange JM, Wang P, Huang W, Ye Z (2019) Smart healthcare: making medical care more intelligent. Glob Health J 3(3):62–65. https://doi.org/10.1016/j.glohj.2019.07.001
66. La Vattiata FC (2023) AI systems involved in harmful events: liable persons or mere instruments? An interdisciplinary and comparative analysis. BioLaw J Rivista di BioDiritto 1:485–499. https://doi.org/10.15168/2284-4503-2646
67. Lagioia F, Sartor G (2020) AI systems under criminal law: a legal analysis and a regulatory perspective. Philos Technol 33(3):433–465. https://doi.org/10.1007/s13347-019-00362-x
68. Castiglioni I, Rundo L, Codari M, Di Leo G, Salvatore C, Interlenghi M et al (2021) AI applications to medical images: from machine learning to deep learning. Phys Med 83:9–24. https://doi.org/10.1016/j.ejmp.2021.02.006
69. Roberts DA, Yaida S, Hanin B (2022) The principles of deep learning theory. Cambridge University Press, Cambridge, p 9
70. Sejnowski TJ (2020) The unreasonable effectiveness of deep learning in artificial intelligence. Proceed Natl Acad Sci 117(48):30033–30038. https://doi.org/10.1073/pnas.1907373117
71. Guembe B, Azeta A, Misra S, Osamor VC, Fernandez-Sanz L, Pospelova V (2022) The emerging threat of AI-driven cyber attacks: a review. Appl Artif Intell 36(1):2037254. https://doi.org/10.1080/08839514.2022.2037254
72. Sangwan RS, Badr Y, Srinivasan SM (2023) Cybersecurity for AI systems: a survey. J Cybersec Priv 3(2):166–190. https://doi.org/10.3390/jcp3020010
73. Yamin MM, Ullah M, Ullah H, Katt B (2021) Weaponized AI for cyber attacks. J Inform Sec Appl 57:102722. https://doi.org/10.1016/j.jisa.2020.102722
74. Mei A (2023) Unveiling covert threats: towards physically safe and transparent AI systems (Doctoral dissertation, University of California, Santa Barbara)
75. Urbas G (2021) Legal considerations in the use of artificial intelligence in the investigation of online child exploitation. In: ANU college of law research paper. https://doi.org/10.2139/ssrn.3978325
76. Aires de Sousa S (2022) Connections (and limits) between law and natural sciences: the concepts of causality and culpability from the perspective of criminal law. Int J Semiot Law Revue internationale de Sémiotique juridique 35(1):287–296. https://doi.org/10.1007/s11196-020-09788-5
77. Makturidi MG, Rusyana AY, Ahyani H (2022) Analisis Deterministik Kausal Secara Sosial yang Menyebabkan Pertanggungjawaban Pidana di Era 4.0. PAMALI Pattimura Magister Law Rev 2(1):17–42. https://doi.org/10.47268/pamali.v2i1.711.
78. Chandra R, Sanjaya K (2023) Punishing the unpunishable: a liability framework for artificial intelligence systems. In: International conference on digital technologies and applications. Springer, Cham, pp 55–64. https://doi.org/10.1007/978-3-031-29860-8_6

79. Kingston JK (2016) Artificial intelligence and legal liability. In: Research and development in intelligent systems XXXIII: incorporating applications and innovations in intelligent systems XXIV 33. Springer, New York, pp 269–279. https://doi.org/10.1007/978-3-319-47175-4_20
80. Kirpichnikov D, Pavlyuk A, Grebneva Y, Okagbue H (2020) Criminal liability of the artificial intelligence. In: E3S web of conferences, vol 159. EDP Sciences, p 04025. https://doi.org/10.1051/e3sconf/202015904025
81. Gless S, Silverman E, Weigend T (2016) If robots cause harm, who is to blame? Self-driving cars and criminal liability. New Crim Law Rev 19(3):412–436. https://doi.org/10.1525/nclr.2016.19.3.412
82. Dai D, Boroomand S (2021) A review of artificial intelligence to enhance the security of big data systems: state-of-art, methodologies, applications, and challenges. Arch Comput Methods Eng 21:1–19. https://doi.org/10.1007/s11831-021-09628-0
83. Zelinka I, Šenkeřík R (2020) Swarm intelligence in cybersecurity. In: Proceedings of the 2020 genetic and evolutionary computation conference companion, pp 1313–1342. https://doi.org/10.1145/3377929.3389851
84. Ali A, Ghouri KFK, Naseem H, Soomro TR, Mansoor W, Momani AM (2022) Battle of deep fakes: artificial intelligence set to become a major threat to the individual and national security. In: Proceedings of the 2022 international conference on cyber resilience (ICCR). IEEE, pp 1–5. https://doi.org/10.1109/ICCR56254.2022.9995821
85. Bazarkina D (2023) Current and future threats of the malicious use of artificial intelligence by terrorists: psychological aspects. In: The Palgrave handbook of malicious use of AI and psychological security. Springer, Cham, pp. 251–272. https://doi.org/10.1007/978-3-031-22552-9_10
86. Gradoń K (2020) Crime in the time of the plague: Fake news pandemic and the challenges to law-enforcement and intelligence community. Soc Reg 4(2):133–148
87. Perez-Des Rosiers D (2021) AI application in surveillance for public safety: adverse risks for contemporary societies. In: Keskin T, Kiggins RD (eds) Towards an international political economy of artificial intelligence. international political economy series. Palgrave Macmillan, Cham. https://doi.org/10.1007/978-3-030-74420-5_6
88. Stone P, Brooks R, Brynjolfsson E, Calo R, Etzioni O, Hager G et al (2022) Artificial intelligence and life in 2030: the one hundred year study on artificial intelligence. arXiv preprint arXiv:2211.06318. https://doi.org/10.48550/arXiv.2211.06318
89. Ahmad MA, Eckert C, Teredesai A (2019) The challenge of imputation in explainable artificial intelligence models. arXiv preprint arXiv:1907.12669. https://doi.org/10.48550/arXiv.1907.12669
90. King TC, Aggarwal N, Taddeo M, Floridi L (2020) Artificial intelligence crime: an interdisciplinary analysis of foreseeable threats and solutions. Sci Eng Ethics 26:89–120. https://doi.org/10.1007/s11948-018-00081-0
91. Jakobs G (2004) Imputation in criminal law and the conditions for norm validity. Buffalo Crim Law Rev 7(2):491–511. https://doi.org/10.1525/nclr.2004.7.2.491
92. Simmler M (2020) The importance of placing blame: criminal law and the stabilization of norms. In: Criminal law forum, vol 31. Springer, New York, pp 147–178. https://doi.org/10.1007/s10609-020-09390-1
93. Toepel F (2012) The fault element in the history of German criminal theory: With some general conclusions for the rules of imputation in a legal system. Crim Law Philos 6:167–186. https://doi.org/10.1007/s11572-012-9150-4
94. Mosechkin IN (2019) Artificial intelligence and criminal liability: problems of becoming a new type of crime subject. Vestnik Saint Petersburg UL, p 461. https://doi.org/10.21638/spbu14.2019.304
95. Glavaničová D, Pascucci M (2022) Vicarious liability: a solution to a problem of AI responsibility? Ethics Inform Technol 24(3):28. https://doi.org/10.1007/s10676-022-09657-8
96. Lima G, Cha M, Jeon C, Park KS (2021) The conflict between people's urge to punish AI and legal systems. Front Robot AI 8:756242. https://doi.org/10.3389/frobt.2021.756242

97. Dongmei P, Olkhovik NV (2022) Criminal liability for actions of artificial intelligence: approach of Russia and China. https://doi.org/10.17516/1997-1370-0912
98. Trinh TV (2019) Models of criminal liability of artificial intelligence: from science fiction to prospect for criminal law and policy in Vietnam. VNU J Sci Legal Stud 35(4):4257
99. Custers B (2022) AI in criminal law: an overview of AI applications in substantive and procedural criminal law. In: Law and artificial intelligence: regulating AI and applying AI in legal practice, pp 205–223. https://doi.org/10.1007/978-94-6265-523-2_11
100. Sumantri VK (2019) Legal responsibility on errors of the artificial intelligence-based robots. Lentera Hukum 6:337
101. Sibai FN (2020) AI crimes: a classification. In: Proceedings of the 2020 international conference on cyber security and protection of digital services (cyber security). IEEE, pp 1–8. https://doi.org/10.1109/CyberSecurity49315.2020.9138891
102. Badar ME (2005) Mens rea-mistake of law & (and) mistake of fact in german criminal law: a survey for international criminal tribunals. Int'l Crim L Rev 5:203. https://doi.org/10.1163/1571812054127790
103. Simester AP (1992) Mistakes in defence. Oxford J Legal Stud 12(2):295–310
104. Simons KW (2009) Mistake of fact or mistake of criminal law? Explaining and defending the distinction. Crim Law Philos 3:213–239. https://doi.org/10.1007/s11572-009-9071-z
105. Simester A (2021) Fundamentals of criminal law: responsibility, culpability, and wrongdoing. Oxford University Press, Oxford, P 231
106. Chiesa LE (2014) Reassessing professor Dressler's Plea for complicity reform: lessons from civil law jurisdictions. New Eng J Crim Civ Confin 40:1
107. Mañalich JP (2020) The abandonment of a criminal attempt as imputable avoidance or prevention of the Offense's consummation El desistimiento de la tentativa como evitación o impedimento imputable de la consumación. https://doi.org/10.4067/S0718-33992020000200780
108. Burke JM (2014) Mistake of fact/mistake of law. Encycl Criminol Crim Just 12:1–5. https://doi.org/10.1002/9781118517383.wbeccj534
109. Wilberg H (2019) Re-evaluating mistake of fact as a ground of review. Available at SSRN 4167374. https://doi.org/10.2139/ssrn.4167374
110. Dezember A, Luna S, Woestehoff SA, Stoltz M, Manley M, Quas JA, Redlich AD (2022) Plea validity in circuit court: judicial colloquies in misdemeanor vs. felony charges. Psychol Crime Law 28(3):268–288. https://doi.org/10.1080/1068316X.2021.1905813
111. Goebel J (2016) Felony and misdemeanor: a study in the history of criminal law. University of Pennsylvania Press
112. Dimock S (2013) Actio libera in causa. Crim Law Philos 7:549–569. https://doi.org/10.1007/s11572-013-9245-6
113. Fernández Ruiz JM (2021) Criteria for evaluation of the type and exception models in the actio libera in causa. Opin Juríd 20(41):49–70. https://doi.org/10.22395/ojum.v20n41a1.
114. Lederman E (1985) Criminal law, perpetrator and corporation: rethinking a complex triangle. J Crim Law Criminol 76(2):285–340. https://doi.org/10.2307/1143611
115. Spencer JR, Brajeux M-A (2010) Criminal liability for negligence—a lesson from across the channel? Int Comp Law Quart 59(1):1–24
116. Balcerzak T, Sieradzka M (2022) Polish criminal liability of the UAV operator in connection with the unauthorized flight in operations area of fire services in the context of the possibility of the U-space using. J Intell Robot Syst 106(1):25. https://doi.org/10.1007/s10846-022-01727-9
117. Barfield W (2018) Liability for autonomous and artificially intelligent robots. Paladyn J Behav Robot 9(1):193–203. https://doi.org/10.1515/pjbr-2018-0018
118. Lederman J, Garrett M, Taylor BD (2016) Fault-y reasoning: navigating the liability terrain in intelligent transportation systems. Public Works Manag Policy 21(1):5–27. https://doi.org/10.1177/1087724X15592891
119. Badue C, Guidolini R, Carneiro RV, Azevedo P, Cardoso VB, Forechi A et al (2021) Self-driving cars: a survey. Exp Syst Appl 165:113816. https://doi.org/10.1016/j.eswa.2020.113816

120. Kuutti S, Bowden R, Jin Y, Barber P, Fallah S (2020) A survey of deep learning applications to autonomous vehicle control. IEEE Trans Intell Transp Syst 22(2):712–733. https://doi.org/10.1109/TITS.2019.2962338
121. Fayyad J, Jaradat MA, Gruyer D, Najjaran H (2020) Deep learning sensor fusion for autonomous vehicle perception and localization: a review. Sensors 20(15):4220. https://doi.org/10.3390/s20154220
122. Muhammad K, Ullah A, Lloret J, Del Ser J, de Albuquerque VHC (2020) Deep learning for safe autonomous driving: current challenges and future directions. IEEE Trans Intell Transp Syst 22(7):4316–4336. https://doi.org/10.1109/TITS.2020.3032227
123. Franklin M, Ashton H, Awad E, Lagnado D (2022) Causal framework of artificial autonomous agent responsibility. In: Proceedings of the 2022 AAAI/ACM conference on AI, ethics, and society, pp 276–284. https://doi.org/10.1145/3514094.3534140
124. Liepiņa R, Wyner A, Sartor G, Lagioia F (2023) Argumentation schemes for legal presumption of causality. In: Proceedings of the nineteenth international conference on artificial intelligence and law, pp 157–166. https://doi.org/10.1145/3594536.3595130
125. Giannini A, Kwik J (2023) Negligence failures and negligence fixes. A comparative analysis of criminal regulation of AI and autonomous vehicles. In: Criminal law forum. Springer, Dordrecht, pp 1–43. https://doi.org/10.1007/s10609-023-09451-1
126. Acquaviva G (2023) Crimes without humanity? Artificial intelligence, meaningful human control, and international criminal law. J Int Crim Just 23:mqad024. https://doi.org/10.1093/jicj/mqad024
127. Bharadiya JP (2023) Machine learning and AI in business intelligence: trends and opportunities. Int J Comput 48(1):123–134
128. O'Leary DE (2013) Artificial intelligence and big data. IEEE Intell Syst 28(2):96–99. https://doi.org/10.1109/MIS.2013.39
129. Huxley-Binns R (2009) When is negligence a crime? Br J Nurs 18(14):892–893
130. Nakar S, Weinberger S, Greenbaum D (2015) Legal and social implications of predictive brain machine interfaces: duty of care, negligence, and criminal responsibility. AJOB Neurosci 6(4):40–42. https://doi.org/10.1080/21507740.2015.1094558
131. Chaudhary G (2020) Artificial intelligence: the liability paradox. ILI Law Rev. https://doi.org/10.2139/ssrn.3709095
132. Hacker P (2023) The European AI liability directives: critique of a half-hearted approach and lessons for the future. Comput Law Sec Rev 51:105871. https://doi.org/10.1016/j.clsr.2023.105871
133. Hallevy G (2015) Liability for crimes involving artificial intelligence systems, vol 257. Springer, New York, pp 29–45
134. Mezrich JL (2022) Is artificial intelligence (AI) a pipe dream? Why legal issues present significant hurdles to AI autonomy. Am J Roentgenol 219(1):152–156. https://doi.org/10.2214/AJR.21.27224
135. Price WN, Gerke S, Cohen IG (2022) Liability for use of artificial intelligence in medicine. In: Nicholson Price W, Gerke S, Glenn Cohen I (eds) Liability for use of artificial intelligence in medicine, research handbook on health, AI and the law, Barry Solaiman and I. Glenn Cohen. Edward Elgar Publishing Ltd. https://doi.org/10.2139/ssrn.4115538
136. Bokhan AP, Petrasheva NV (2016) Complicity in negligent crime: myth or reality? Lex Russica 5:217–224
137. Hamdorf K (2007) The concept of a joint criminal enterprise and domestic modes of liability for parties to a crime: a comparison of German and English law. J Int Crim Just 5(1):208–226. https://doi.org/10.1093/jicj/mql084
138. Ohlin JD (2009) Joint criminal confusion. New Crim Law Rev 12(3):406–419. https://doi.org/10.1525/nclr.2009.12.3.406
139. Romeo-Stuppy K, Béguinot E, De Kanter W (2022) Criminal liability for tobacco corporations and executives. https://doi.org/10.1136/tobaccocontrol-2021-056573
140. Viscusi WK, Moore MJ (1993) Product liability, research and development, and innovation. J Polit Econ 101(1):161–184

141. Guo J, Martinez-Garcia M (2021) Key technologies towards smart manufacturing based on swarm intelligence and edge computing. Comput Electr Eng 92:107119. https://doi.org/10.1016/j.compeleceng.2021.107119
142. Pham QV, Nguyen DC, Mirjalili S, Hoang DT, Nguyen DN, Pathirana PN, Hwang WJ (2021) Swarm intelligence for next-generation networks: recent advances and applications. J Netw Comput Appl 191:103141. https://doi.org/10.1016/j.jnca.2021.103141
143. Ohlin J (2021) Complicity, negligence, and command responsibility. Temple Int Compar Law J 35(1):109–120
144. Padovan PH, Martins CM, Reed C (2023) Black is the new orange: how to determine AI liability. Artif Intell Law 31(1):133–167. https://doi.org/10.1007/s10506-022-09308-9

Chapter 2
Theoretical Preconditions of Criminal Imputation for Negligence Crime Involving AI

2.1 Different Theoretical Efforts to Address the Challenges of the Imputation Gaps

With the characteristics of AI technology, the criminal imputation for the negligence crime involving AI has challenged the traditional imputation theory, which creates a gap in criminal imputation that results from the inability to attribute criminal liability to the appropriate subject of the criminal liability. In order to cope with such challenges, the theory has been working in two main directions to fill the imputation gap: first, the legislative direction of adding AI crimes to the criminal law and the countermeasure direction of establishing the AI criminal law system. Although these two theoretical efforts have various theoretical and practical shortcomings in filling the criminal imputation gap, they provide possibility for discussion on the reasonable criminal imputation. Therefore, it is a sound choice to discuss these theoretical endeavors in detail before arguing for the theoretical premises of imputation for the negligence crime involving AI.

2.1.1 Legislative Efforts to Stipulate Crimes Involving AI in Criminal Law

In recent years, AI has woven itself into our daily lives in ways we may not even be aware of. It has become so pervasive that many remain unaware of both its impact and our reliance upon it [1–3]. Therefore, with the increasing penetration of AI into today's social life and its inherent technical risks, this has indeed had a certain impact on the application of criminal law norms. Some studies believe that this impact is mainly reflected in the fact that the liability principles established by criminal law norms and numerous offences cannot effectively regulate crimes involving AI [4, 5].

S. Zhao, *Principle of Criminal Imputation for Negligence Crime Involving Artificial Intelligence*, Artificial Intelligence and the Rule of Law,
https://doi.org/10.1007/978-981-97-0722-5_2

Therefore, if current criminal law norms are used to regulate such crimes involving AI, there will inevitably be inappropriate convictions and sentencing for these crimes. However, the majority of studies continue to argue that although crimes involving AI have caused some impact on the application of criminal law norms, such impact has not shaken the foundation and framework of the existing criminal law norms. Therefore, only partial adjustments to the criminal law norms are needed to deal with this problem [5–7].

Specifically, the legislative efforts are mainly found in the following two aspects: first, the liability principles stipulated in the existing criminal law are unable to meet the demands of imputation for the negligence crime involving AI. As a result, the imputation gaps brought about by negligence crimes involving AI are mainly found in the general provisions of the criminal law norms [6, 8, 9], secondly, the offences stipulated in the specific provisions of criminal law cannot reasonably evaluate the negligence crimes involving AI, and the penalties cannot properly meet the new requirements for the imputation for such crimes. Therefore, the gaps in the criminal imputation are mainly related to the specific provisions of the criminal law.

To this end, such legislative efforts to deal with the gaps in the imputation for negligence crime involving AI have focused on the following aspects.

Firstly, the subject of such crime can only be a natural person and not an AI. In the criminal law theory, the criminal subject typically refers to the individual who has committed a crime, also known as the offender or the perpetrator [9, 10]. The criminal subject is the person responsible for engaging in actions or behaviors that are prohibited by criminal law, leading to legal consequences such as fines, probation, imprisonment, or other forms of punishment. In the crimes involving AI, AI has never isolated from its own tool attributes [11, 12]. It does not have the independent will and ability to identify and control something. Therefore, AI can only be used as an object of the crime and cannot become the subject of criminal liability. For the negligence crime involving AI, criminal liability can ultimately only be attributed to the natural person rather than AI. To put it simply, in crimes involving AI, artificial intelligence cannot be the subject of crimes, so it cannot be the object of criminal imputation.

Secondly, the criminal law should stipulate the strict liability for crimes involving AI. In the criminal practice, most crimes require prosecutors to establish mens rea, or a guilty mind, in order to prove a defendant is guilty of a crime [13]. In contrast, strict liability crimes do not require the defendant to have a culpable mental state of mind when committing the crime to be guilty. In fact, such liability is generally limited to minor offenses, such as misdemeanors and infractions. In the nineteenth century, strict liability laws were created in Britain in order to improve working and safety standards in factories [14, 15]. Needing to prove mens rea on the part of the factory owners was very difficult and resulted in very few prosecutions. The creation of strict liability offenses meant that convictions were increased. Common strict liability offenses today include the selling of alcohol to underage persons and statutory rape [16, 17].

With regard to the crimes involving AI, some researchers have argued that the stipulation principle for the negligent crime in the criminal law can no longer meet the demand for imputation for such crime involving AI, and have therefore advocated the establishment of strict liability in the criminal law for the imputation for such crimes [18–20]. However, in the criminal imputation for the negligence crime, which person should bear such strict liability? There stand different theoretical views on this. One of the views suggests that AI designers, producers, owners, and users may all have possibility to bear the strict liability [21, 22]. For example, in the case of a traffic accident caused by self-driving vehicles, the user does not have the obligation to foresee the result since he did not participate in the driving behavior of the autonomous driving model. However, according to the principle of strict liability, the owner, manufacturer or program designer of the self-driving car should bear the strict liability for the traffic accident. However, in the case of a self-driving mode in which the user is partially involved in the driving behavior, the user can exclude his obligation of care because he is not fully involved in the driving [21]. If the user fails to take timely and effective braking measures to prevent the result from occurring when an emergency situation arises during use, he shall bear the negligence liability for this traffic accidents according to strict liability [23–25].

Contrary to this common view of strict liability, another view is that the designer of self-driving cars should be held liable for fault, while the producer should be held strictly liable [26, 27]. In the case of AI technology, its corresponding research and development before the market application is only the result of laboratory work, while its market application is in fact the beginning of the real life of the technology. Precisely for this reason, we should take tolerant and open attitude to the scientific research and product development. Only in this way, scientists can purely conduct research and experiment, so the people concerned should not be held criminally liable at this stage of product development. However, when the AI product enters the market is applicated, the technology and the product will undoubtedly pose certain risks [28, 29]. In this regard, if the maker of the product does not maintain the duty of care, then corresponding products can bring a lot of harm in the market application. Therefore, the strict liability of the product maker is also a way to reduce the risk posed by the AI products with its market application [30, 31].

Finally, some scholars advocate adding some new offence involving AI in the criminal law. In response to the criminal imputation gap created by AI, some have argued that we can through legislation directly stipulate the new offences in the criminal code, which would allow for a more rational response to the risks posed by the crimes involving AI [6, 32, 33]. Such offences to be stipulated in the criminal law fall into the following main categories: the first is the crime of illegal use of AI. In the case of malicious use of AI, the act is a serious danger to the society and therefore has the necessity to impose the penal punishment [34, 35]. In practice, the malicious use of AI to commit some specific crimes is increasing year by year. In order to regulate the preparatory act for this malicious use of AI, which cannot be evaluated in terms of perpetrating act, there is a need to stipulate such preparatory acts as one specific offense. In essence, such malicious use of AI is a preparatory act for a subsequent crime. Therefore, the stipulation of a separate crime for such act is the criminalization of preparatory acts in the criminal law [36, 37].

Another crime that should be additionally stipulated in the criminal law is the crime of major safety accidents with AI. It is generally recognized that when AI is widely used in various areas of public safety, there is a risk that it will get out of control and finally lead to major accidents involving severe injuries, deaths, or great losses of public and private properties [38, 39]. If the accident was caused by the failure of the designer, user or person concerned with AI to comply with the regulations of AI, such person should be penalized by this crime. In addition to these crimes with major accidents, some have suggested stimulating the crime of dereliction of duty by state personnel organs in the regulation of the use of AI, thereby increasing the responsibility of such personnel in the regulation of the use of AI [40, 41].

The above legislative efforts have, on the one hand, enhanced the possibility of criminal law to effectively regulate the corresponding crimes involving AI and, on the other hand, ensured the overall stability of criminal law norms and criminal law theories. Although there is obvious rationality in these efforts, this theoretical effort also has many negative effects. Specifically, by introducing the strict liability, this legislative effort attempts to reduce the consideration of imputation factors such as foreseeability and causation that are difficult to ascertain in the criminal imputation for the crimes involving AI. With regard to the strict liability, the penalty is imposed on the perpetrator in the practice as long as it is proved that the perpetrator has committed a certain act or that certain harmful consequences have occurred, regardless of whether or not he is at fault [42]. However, such strict liability applies only to certain misdemeanor, so this does not cause too much injustice objectively. In reality, the majority of crimes involving AI are not these types of misdemeanors, so introducing strict liability in the criminal imputation would instead create much more serious injustice.

Another legislative attempt has been made to criminalize the malicious use of AI in the criminal law. In essence, this kind of legislative effort is to achieve the early intervention of criminal law in citizens' behavior by using the elements of abstract dangerous crimes. This is bound to greatly reduce the space for civil rights. With regard to the legislative efforts to stipulate the corresponding crime of major safety accidents and crime of dereliction of duty, the existing relevant criminal law provisions are in fact fully capable of providing a reasonable response to such crimes involving AI, and there is no need to provide for some specific provisions in this regard. In addition, stipulating this new offense in the criminal law will undoubtedly expand the current criminal circle, which will have the negative consequence of causing inconvenience the lives of ordinary people through the excessive interference of penalties in their lives. It can be seen that such various legislative efforts are not a reasonable direction in dealing with the criminal imputation challenges posed by crimes involving AI.

2.1.2 Efforts to Establish the Specific AI Criminal Law System

Since the criminal risks derived from the application of AI technology have a structural impact on the application of criminal law, it is partly argued that neither the existing criminal law norms nor the traditional criminal law theories can effectively cope with the gaps in criminal imputation for the crimes involving AI [4, 43]. On this premise, some discussions have argued that only the establishment of an AI criminal law system can thoroughly and effectively address this imputation challenge.

This view to establish AI criminal law system is mainly based on the following premise: the risk posed by AI technology application is different from any previous social risk, and its impact on social life and the legal system can hardly be eliminated through the traditional countermeasures [44–46]. Accordingly, the characteristics of AI technology and the criminal risks it brings have caused the decisive impact on many aspects of traditional criminal law norms and theories [12, 47].

Specifically, the first is about the subject of the crime. With the development and application of AI technology, the future AI product will form the same thought process and free will as that of the natural person through its in-depth learning, so it has met all the conditions to become the subject of the crime [48, 49]. Therefore, AI can become the subject of crime, and when it commits a criminal act as the perpetrator, it also should be punished according to the criminal law [34, 50]. In generally, the company can be regarded as the same criminal subject as natural persons, so there is no theoretical obstacle to treating AI as a criminal subject in criminal law theory. With this in mind, the development of AI has changed the structure and composition of the crime subject.

In addition, the development and application of AI has changed the traditional concept of actus reus in criminal law. According to the general understanding in the theory, actus reus has three basic characteristics: first, it is controlled by the human will; second, it is capable of changing and affecting the objective things; and third, it is expressly prohibited by the criminal law [51, 52]. However, according to the understanding of AI criminal law system, the behavior of AI should be regulated by criminal law. This understanding inevitably involves a breakthrough in the attribute that behavior is "controlled by human will." Finally, the traditional penalty system is constructed on the natural persons. Therefore, both retributive and preventive penalties are based on the premise that natural persons have the ability to take responsibility, but AI, as a collection of software and hardware, does not have the ability to take responsibility because it does not have the perception of human beings [53, 54].

It is with these prerequisite considerations that some opinions advocate the establishment of the specific AI criminal law system in the three aspects: subject of crime, actus reus, and penalty system, so as to be able to effectively and reasonably cope with the criminal imputation gaps. In terms of subject of crime, this view abandons the theoretical tradition that such subject can only be composed of the natural person. This view holds that AI can have its own will after it develops to a certain stage, and the behavior it implements is not the will of the programmer, but of the AI [49, 54]. Moreover, AI has the capacity for the criminal responsibility, which consists of the ability to recognize and control his behavior, and thus the AI can be punished according to the criminal law. Although such view adheres to the traditional theory of criminal imputation, in the allocation of responsibility, the theorists of this viewpoint advocate that AI and natural persons can commit a joint crime [55, 56]. In this case, AI and natural persons are convicted and sentenced according to the subjective and objective factors and their participation in the joint crime. Although this view regards AI as the same criminal subject as natural persons, the punishment for AI cannot be the same as that for the natural persons. Therefore, this view advocates the addition of punishment measures such as deletion of data, modification of programs, permanent destruction, etc., for the intelligent robots in the criminal law [57, 58].

From the perspective of establishing AI criminal law system, only by fundamentally changing the theory of subject, actus reus, and penalty in the criminal law can we effectively deal with the gaps in the imputation for the crime involving AI. While it is true that this effort can provide a targeted response to the difficulties of imputation that arise from AI-related crimes, the fact that it completely abandons traditional theories of criminal subject, actus rues, and punishment is not always a positive result. For example, according to this view, AI, like natural person, needs to bear corresponding criminal liability as criminal subject. However, how to protect the interest of AI from criminal law? In other words, if infringement has been committed against AI, how should this behavior should be dealt with according to the criminal law? In this regard, this view does not address how to give the criminal law protection to AI even though it is dealt with as subject of crime.

On the other hand, if the AI criminal law system is established, what is the relationship between this system and the traditional criminal law system? If this is not thoroughly resolved, then the result will inevitably lead to confusion in criminal law theory, which will not only be detrimental to the resolution of the criminal imputation for the crimes involving AI, but will also affect the effective and rational response of criminal law to a large number of traditional crimes [59–62]. Finally, the direction of such theoretical effort to make AI liable for criminal punishment as subject of crime is more of a choice to appease public sentiment in the society. Regarding the criminal law system, the rational choice in the practice is more about the effect of the application of penalties rather than the appeasement of public sentiment. It is because it overly meets the demands of the public to punish certain behaviors that undoubtedly squeezes the space for criminal law to rationally respond to crime, thus creating the danger of criminal law becoming an instrument [63–65].

2.2 Theoretical Issues Arising from Such Different Efforts

In view of the gaps in the imputation for the negligence crime involving AI, theoretically, efforts should be made to provide effective and reasonable responses from such two directions: legislation and the establishment of an AI criminal law system.

Although these efforts are reasonable in terms of criminal subjects, strict liability, specific offense, and penalty systems, the negative impact they bring is just the fact. For example, treating AI as subject of crime has a negative impact on the traditional criminal law theory. Thus, after describing the essential elements of these theoretical efforts, a rational evaluation of them from a theoretical standpoint is to provide a basis for criticism of the theoretical premises for later arguments to solve the imputation gaps.

First of all, as far as the creation of the crime of unlawful use of AI in the criminal law is concerned, this legislative proposition is to regard the crime here as an abstract dangerous crime. According to criminal law theory, this type of crime does not require the occurrence of specific harmful consequences to be established. Due to the breadth and seriousness of the harmful consequences of crimes involving AI, the view of responding to them by legislating abstract dangerous crimes will objectively react to the tendency to marginalize the significance of infringement results when responding to crimes involving artificial intelligence. In other words, infringement results are no longer the necessary condition for the establishment and attribution of liability for crimes involving AI. The marginalization of the infringement result reflects the cardinal direction of the legislative response: the establishment of crime of illegal use of AI is based on the act of the perpetrator rather than the harmful result, which indicates that the legislative response to crimes involving AI has shifted from a result-based to a behavior-based approach in criminal law.

Furthermore, this legislative response demonstrates the emphasis of criminal law norms on the protection of collective legal interests. Because the harmful results of AI-related crimes tend to have a wide range of effects and such results tend to be more abstract, the legislative response prefers to abandon the actual harmful result as a condition for the establishment of crimes involving AI. Finally, such legislative response also shows that criminal law norms advance the protection of legal interests, and its purpose is to avoid the occurrence of serious harmful consequences of crimes involving AI to the greatest extent. Although the legislative response has endeavored to address the gap in the imputation for crime involving AI by establishing a small number of offenses, its theoretical direction is in fact fundamental departure from the traditional criminal law theories, and this can bring about a variety of negative impacts on the application of criminal law in the practice.

Secondly, with regard to the forms of liability for crime involving AI, the legislative efforts have been made to establish strict liability with respect to the forms of liability for such crimes. However, strict liability deviates from the liability principle in the criminal law to some extent, which undoubtedly has a great negative impact on the application of criminal law in the practice. In the criminal law theory, criminal liability refers to when a person can be held legally responsible for breaking the law [66, 67]. Such liability includes potential or actual responsibility, which means that a person can be charged and sentenced if he actually committed a crime, or if he is suspected of committing a crime. Therefore, the premise for the offender to bear criminal liability is that he has the ability to take responsibility and has committed the corresponding act intentionally or negligently.

The principle of liability, as a necessary condition for the perpetrator to constitute a crime and assume responsibility, is universal and global in criminal law. However, in the case of negligence crime involving AI, due to the increasing difficulty in examining the subjective factors of the perpetrator, the legislative efforts have advocated the establishment of the principle of strict liability in the criminal law, thus realizing the division and attribution of criminal liability to the responsible subject [21, 68]. Substantively, the introduction of strict liability is aimed at attributing criminal liability for the negligence crime involving AI to the appropriate subjects, thereby avoiding the situation where no one bears the responsibility. Since the strict liability is mainly applied for the malum prohibitum, the introduction of strict liability in the criminal law will not bring a decisive impact on the criminal imputation system centered on the principle of liability. However, the negligence crime involving AI is not malum prohibitum, and such crime is becoming more and more common with the widespread application of AI in our daily life.

Finally, the establishment of a specific AI criminal law system could hinder the normal functioning of the criminal law system. Generally speaking, the security of the criminal law system is manifested in two aspects, one of which is the stability of the criminal law system, and the other is the protection of civil liberties by criminal law. In line with this, the criminal law system, on the one hand, maximizes its security through the objectivity and formality of the punishment and, on the other hand, maximizes its purposiveness through a system of perpetrator-oriented sanctions. It can be said that the security of the criminal law system is in fact the point of balance between the punishment of the crime and the protection of the human rights. In dealing with the criminal risks brought about by AI, only by ensuring the security of the criminal law system can we avoid creating new risks while avoiding them.

However, various efforts proposed to solve the gaps in the imputation for the negligence crime involving AI have had more or less impact on the security of the criminal law system. This impact objectively even directly threatens the foundation of the security of this system. The establishment of a specific AI criminal law system is aimed more at playing the role of criminal law in preventing crimes involving AI. As AI brings more and more risks to people in their daily life, criminal legislation continues to push forward the standard of criminal penalty. In the practice, criminal law norms have been deemed to intervene in advance on occasions when the legal interests of individuals have not yet been actually infringed upon. As this preventive response strategy continues to expand the defense line of criminal law, it also poses a severe challenge to the individual freedom of citizens, which undoubtedly impacts the basic concept of traditional criminal law to protect the civil freedoms.

2.3 Theoretical Prerequisites for Reasonable Imputation

With regard to the gaps in the imputation for the negligence crime involving AI, no matter whether there are legislative responses or the establishment of a specific AI criminal law system, these responses have not achieved the expected results, but have caused a lot of confusion and challenges in the criminal theory and practice. Moreover, because such crimes involving AI have their own characteristics that are different from those of traditional crimes. Therefore, in order to resolve the difficulties of imputation for this type of crime, it is first necessary to identify the theoretical premise for the reasonable imputation. It is only on that premise that greater risks can be avoided as a result of an unreasonable system of criminal imputation.

Generally speaking, the prerequisite considerations for dealing with the imputation gaps for the negligence crime involving AI include whether AI can be the subject of crime, what rational attitude the criminal law should have in response to such crimes, and how the criminal law can meet the demands of imputation for the negligent crime involving AI. These three aspects will be discussed and explained in detail as following.

2.3.1 AI Is Not the Subject of Crime

The history of criminal law shows that human beings have always been the center of the criminal law. However, with the development of AI technology, in order to cope with the gaps resulted in the imputation for the negligent crimes involving AI, some scholars advocate abandoning the center of natural person in the criminal law and using AI artificial intelligence as a criminal subject [69–71]. According to this understanding, AI participates in the social relations regulated by criminal law norms as subject of crime [49, 72, 73]. However, a crucial question is whether AI is capable of committing crimes and being held criminally liable as a criminal subject? For AI, no matter from its way of realizing its intelligence, its operation mechanism or its tool attributes, AI is still essentially a tool for our human beings [74, 75]. The essential difference between AI and human beings is not a deficiency that cannot be realized by the current technology, but rather a prerequisite for the existence and development of it [74, 76, 77].

Therefore, it is not reasonable to argue at the factual level that AI can be the subject of a crime by demonstrating its homogeneity or similarity to humans. In fact, the answer to the above question requires determining whether AI has the conditions to become the subject of crime from a normative perspective, and whether it is necessary to treat AI as a criminal subject from a value perspective.

Normative Perspective

The normative answer to the question of whether AI can be the subject of a crime is to determine, whether the AI has the capacity for its criminal responsibility. As a rule, there is no crime without actus reus, and criminal responsibility does not naturally arise without crime, so that the reality of criminal responsibility is based on conduct in the sense of criminal law [78, 79]. Philosophically, the basis of the criminal responsibility is the free will that natural persons possess [80, 81]. In addition, the assumption of criminal responsibility by the perpetrator implies that he bears the penalty. In this case, the subject who bears criminal responsibility must have the ability to bear such responsibility [82, 83]. It is thus clear that there is no way to discuss the subject of crime from a normative perspective that bypasses the discussion of free will, capacity for responsibility, ability to behavior, and the ability to bear punishment. Similarly, the following will also discuss whether the AI can become the subject of crime from these four aspects.

First, AI does not have free will. Free will determines to some extent whether a person is capable of committing a crime and taking the corresponding criminal responsibility. Therefore, free will is an important reference point for discussing whether AI can become a criminal subject. Does man have free will or not? Regarding this issue, one philosophical view is that everything that is subject to causality is inevitable and determined, and therefore people who are dominated by causality naturally do not have free will [84, 85]. According to the latest brain science research, it has been found that all the mental work done by the human brain is actually the product of neurobiological processes in the brain. Thus, the way and manner in which each person makes decisions and their outcomes depend entirely on how its respective brain is structured and on how its brain processes the corresponding information. In other words, it is not free will, but rather the structure of each person's brain that controls his behavior and makes his decisions [86, 87].

In contrast to the insights of those brain scientists, most philosophers believe that people have free will [88, 89]. They argue that if the opinions of person have long been prescribed by the purely biological structures in the brain, then no one is responsible for what he does anymore. In principle, even a ruthless murderer can borrow this idea to justify himself by pointing out that he did not intend to do it, but that his brain structure compelled him to do it. Objectively, free will is essentially manifested in the fact that a person has achievable independent choices within certain limits. However, AI does not have this ability to make its autonomous choices even within certain limits. From a technical point of view, the realistic path of AI cannot truly give it real human thinking. In fact, AI can only simulate a certain aspect of human intelligence, so its functions are only fully controlled by human design and programming. In this case, AI is in fact determined by human beings and has no possibility of its independent choice. Furthermore, although AI has some technical features such as autonomous control and deep learning, the realization of these features still relies on the empowerment of human technology [90, 91]. Indeed, deep learning does enable AI to acquire capabilities beyond the details of programming, but this does not mean that AI can realize its autonomous choices. AI is essentially a machine made by humans that does not have a biological vector. In the absence of will-dependent biological attributes, it is impossible for AI to produce will like human being.

Second, AI lacks the capacity for responsibility. In the criminal law, the capacity for responsibility refers to a natural person's ability to recognize and control his own behaviors, as well as his ability to take his criminal responsibility [92]. If the perpetrator has ability to recognize something, it means that he is able to recognize the meaning, nature, and consequences of his actions. In the practice, with the help of advanced information collection equipment, AI is completely able to identify the nature, meaning and consequences of its own actions, and may even be more accurate than humans in understanding the possibility of the consequences of actions [93, 94]. Therefore, artificial intelligence has the same ability to recognize something as human beings. In the practice, AI can not only collect a large amount of information, including sounds, images, and smells, through the configuration of information-gathering devices, but also obtain this information to a degree of accuracy that exceeds the ability of human sensory capabilities. However, AI's understanding of such information is at best a factual statistical discovery, which does not mean that it has achieved a normative understanding of its own behavior [95].

In the criminal law, a perpetrator's ability to recognize something means that he is able to understand and identify the social significance of his actions. Although AI is capable of performing certain activities or making certain expressions, these activities and expressions are mechanically matched on the basis of simple formal logic, and it does not have any knowledge of the meaning and nature of its own activities and expressions. As a result, AI only has a so-called perception of its own activities and their corresponding expressions at the factual level, but lacks knowledge of their nature and meaning. Therefore, AI does not have the ability to recognize them in the criminal law.

In addition, the capacity of control in the criminal law refers to the ability of the perpetrator to control his own behavior. Some argue that AI has owned the same ability to control as the natural person. According to this understanding, AI will form powerful analytical capabilities based on its computing power that far exceeds that of humans. Therefore, AI is fully capable of controlling its own behavior [96, 97]. In practice, through computation and analysis, AI has the ability to control its own behavior to make it adapted to specific situations. For example, self-driving cars are able to accurately calculate how many traffic signals are within a few kilometers, as well as determine its exact speed, make judgments about the obstacles and then decide how to effectively avoid vehicles and pedestrians [98]. In the criminal law, the ability to control is specifically reflected in whether the perpetrator chooses to violate the criminal law norms. In other words, it is whether the perpetrator has control over his illegal behavior. In a normative sense, the ability to control lies in the fact that the perpetrator understands and controls his violation of criminal law norms. Although AI can control its own activities at the factual level, it cannot recognize the normative significance of its own behavior in the same way as a natural person, and therefore it cannot control the elements of the violation at the normative level [99, 100].

In short, even if AI can realize the collection and transmission of information and the corresponding physical control of activities on the factual level, AI has no ability not only to recognize and comply with criminal law norms, but also to perceive the negative consequences of the negative social evaluation caused by violating the norms. Therefore, AI does not have the ability to recognize and control its behavior in the normative sense.

Third, AI lacks the behavioral capability. In addition to the capacity for responsibility, the subject of a crime in criminal law requires that he has the capacity to act. In the practice, someone has his behavioral capability means that he has actual ability to perform a behavior through essential knowledge and skills. In other word, a person must know what to do and how to do if he will successfully perform his behavior [101]. Generally, without act, there is no crime, and naturally, no crime gives rise to criminal responsibility. Therefore, the act has decisive significance for the criminal liability. The capacity to act is the ability of the subject to control his behavior according to his own will. In the case of AI, it does not have the behavioral capability. First, AI lacks the biological nature of human being, and any activity of AI is only the mechanical activity [102, 103]. Secondly, AI carries out its external activities in accordance with the program prepared by the developer, and such program is not essentially the human mind and will, so the activities of the AI under the domination of the program naturally do not belong to the behavior.

In this regard, different views believe that AI can produce its independent thinking and will through its deep learning, and therefore has the same behavioral capability as natural people [104, 105]. However, the deep learning is in fact only an algorithm, which does not endow AI with the same will and thinking as a human being. Therefore, AI does not have the behavioral capability.

Fourth, AI does not have the ability to bear the penalty. Generally speaking, penalty is the sanctions that inflict pain on the offender. The capacity to bear the penalty is the ability of the offender to feel and bear the pain of his penalty. For the offender, his ability to bear punishment requires that he be able to feel the pain of his punishment. At the same time, he is also required to bear the corresponding deprivation of the punishment [106]. Therefore, the ability of the offender to bear penalty can be illustrated from these two aspects. For AI, whether it has this ability can also be explained from these two aspects. First of all, AI cannot perceive the pain caused by the penalty. From the content, the pain of penalty includes the physical pain caused directly or indirectly to the natural person by the penalty, and the emotional pain caused by the deprivation or restriction of the offender's eligibility to engage in social activities as a result of the penalty [107, 108]. In this regard, AI cannot perceive the pain caused by punishment, including free imprisonment, property punishment and qualification punishment. Therefore, it is completely impossible for AI to perceive the pain caused by punishment. In addition, AI has neither freedom rights nor property rights, nor corresponding qualification rights. Therefore, it cannot bear the consequences of punishment like natural persons.

To sum up, from a normative perspective, AI does not have free will, capacity for responsibility, behavioral capability and the ability to bear the penalty, which are the general requirements to be the subject of crime, therefore, AI cannot become a subject of crime.

Value Perspective

In addition to determining normatively whether AI has the same conditions as natural persons to be a subject of crime, it is still necessary to analyze whether AI needs to be a criminal subject from the value perspective, so that it is necessary to use penalty to response to its behavior.

Therefore, the key to judging from the value perspective is whether the impact of crimes involving AI on the traditional criminal law theoretical system is sufficiently serious to the extent that it has already subverted the foundation of the theory, thus requiring the reconstruction of the criminal law theoretical system. As the conclusion has been argued before, the wide application of AI has indeed brought a great impact to the traditional criminal law theory. However, the key question is, is this impact enough to change the traditional criminal law theory and thus give AI the qualifications to be the subject of crime? This can be discussed from the following two aspects. Firstly, rational evaluation of the impact of AI on the criminal law. There is no doubt that crimes involving AI have characteristics that distinguish them from the traditional crimes, and these characteristics have indeed had a certain impact on the application of criminal law theories and norms [37, 109]. However, this impact has not yet reached the level of subversion of the traditional criminal law theories and norms.

In practice, crimes involving AI include various intentional crimes that use AI as criminal tool, as well as negligent crimes that fail to fulfill the obligations of safe production and management of AI. Regardless of intentional or negligent crimes, the criminal law norms can still be applied to these crimes. When these acts have the constitutive elements of crime, it is sufficient to convict and punish them in accordance with the specific provisions of the criminal law. For example, if AI is used to commit murder, injury or fraud, the corresponding behavior may constitute the crime of homicide, injury and fraud. Moreover, failure to fulfill safety production and management obligations for AI may constitute the crime of negligent homicide, the crime of traffic accidents, etc. So far, these crimes involving AI have not exceeded the regulation scope of the criminal law. Therefore. the majority view is that existing criminal law norms are almost adequate to deal with crimes involving AI [19, 110, 111]. As far as the criminal law theories are concerned, the existing theories can still be applied to crimes involving AI.

Despite the gaps in imputation for the negligent crimes involving AI, the traditional criminal law theories, especially the theory of subject of crime, the behavior theory, and the liability theory, are still of great significance to the treatment of such crimes. For example, as to whether AI can constitute the subject of crime, different opinions are still arguing about the two traditional theories of the ability to recognize and to control [46, 90].

Undoubtedly, the rapid advancement and integration of AI have ushered in profound transformations across various spheres of society and the legal landscape. Nevertheless, it is imperative to recognize that this accelerated AI development, while impactful, is unlikely to fundamentally upend the underlying fabric of social relationships or alter their essence [2, 112, 113]. As conventional wisdom dictates, substantial shifts in legal norms are primarily driven by the nature and substance of social connections. Consequently, the emergence and evolution of AI-related criminal activities alone are insufficient to undermine existing criminal law principles and doctrines. Furthermore, the inherent adaptability of legal norms and theories serves to effectively moderate the influence of AI-related crimes, thereby preventing any disruptive effects of this emerging phenomenon on the overall normative and theoretical framework.

In conclusion, despite the existence of the gaps in the imputation for the negligent crimes involving AI in the judicial practice, the existing criminal law norms and traditional criminal law theory can still play an effective role in the norm application and value guidance as a whole. In particular, some basic theories, such as the theory of the criminal subject, are still able to effectively support the establishment and functioning of the criminal law normative system. Hence, a reasoned evaluation of the impact of AI on criminal law theory will indicate that it has not yet reached the point of deconstructing the theoretical underpinnings of criminal law subject theory. The current criminal law theory framework remains capable of addressing and adapting to this influence.

Secondly, the disqualification of AI as a criminal subject based on value judgments. Based on the preceding arguments, the issue of imputation gaps in the crimes involving AI is confined solely to the realm of negligent crimes. Consequently, the theoretical response to this challenge should remain within the confines of negligent crimes, refraining from impacting other normative domains [54, 65, 114, 115]. Therefore, for the view of giving AI the status of a subject of crime, this response will not only shake the basic theory of criminal law, but also create new theoretical challenges while dealing with the gaps in the imputation for the negligent crime involving AI. Based on this consideration, one view is that the imputation gap for crimes involving AI is mainly because the foreseeability in negligence crimes is not available in the negligence crimes involving AI. In the traditional criminal law theory, the perpetrator's foreseeability is the basis for the establishment of negligence crimes. This kind of foresight requires the perpetrator to be able to foresee the relatively specific content such as specific results and causal processes, but this standard of foresight is indeed too high for the perpetrator in the negligence crimes. In addition, the absence of these pre-existing regulations concerning the design, production and use of AI means that there are few standards by which the duty of care can be delineated, which also affects the imputation for the negligence crime involving AI [20, 116–118].

Given these insights, some perspectives argue that AI has not transcended its instrumental nature, lacks independent will, and is incapable of recognition and control of the behavior from the perpetrator. Consequently, it can only be regarded as an object within criminal law, rather than as a subject of crime. In cases of crimes involving artificial intelligence, the assignment of criminal responsibility ultimately pertains solely to natural persons [4]. However, crimes involving AI are, after all, different from the traditional crimes, and therefore require all variations in the imputation for these such crimes. For example, the relevant crimes involving AI will be included in the existing elements of the specific crime, so as to solve the problem of the corresponding behavior cannot be convicted. According to this view, the designers and producers of AI should fulfill the "obligation to ensure product safety" in the process of research, design, production and manufacture of AI. If the relevant persons violate this obligation, they should be convicted in accordance with the crime of producing products that do not comply with safety standards. Furthermore, concerning the potential foreseeability of the perpetrator in crimes involving AI, this perspective maintains that the perpetrator does not need to have the specific foresight of the facts and causality but rather an abstract awareness of the danger [19, 59].

It can be seen that some of the basic problems encountered in the imputation for the negligence involving AI can be solved through the explanation and illustration of existing criminal law theories, so as to reasonably cope with the corresponding imputation gap. Therefore, whether in theory or in practice, it is a rational choice to deal with the imputation gap in negligence crimes involving AI under the existing criminal law theory and normative framework.

With regard to whether AI can become the subject of crime, the above argument clearly shows that: whether from a normative perspective or a value perspective, AI cannot and should not be the subject of crime. In response to the challenge to the traditional criminal law theory and criminal law norms posed by crimes involving AI, adherence to the subject theory of crimes committed by natural persons is a rational choice to cope with this challenge. However, adhering to the traditional criminal law theory does not mean adopting a passive avoidance attitude towards such crimes involving AI. On the contrary, AI needs to find an appropriate foothold within the traditional criminal law norms and theoretical system, so as to provide a more reasonable theoretical and normative basis for rationally responding to the challenges posed by the crimes involving AI. Only in this way can there be room in the criminal law to reasonably respond to the challenges of such crimes involving AI, without shaking the basic criminal law norms and criminal law theory system.

With this consideration, what are the basic concepts that should be held in the criminal law norms as well as the theoretical system in order to cope with such challenges posed by crimes involving AI? This will be mainly argued in the next part of this study.

2.3.2 Conceptual Approaches to Address the Imputation Gaps

In addressing the imputation gaps in negligence crime involving AI, the response from criminal law encompasses not only the exclusion of AI as a subject of crime but also the selection of conceptual approaches to address the challenges posed by AI-related crimes. Within the context of imputation for such crime, the adoption of conceptual options is not only a vital prerequisite for effectively resolving the imputation gaps but also an unavoidable decision for criminal law to address these crimes. Broadly speaking, this choice primarily encompasses the following aspects.

Rational Intervention in Development of AI Technology

As the most severe legal response, criminal law combats crime on the one hand and protects the legal interests on the other, so the impact of criminal law on human beings is often far-reaching. In modern society, criminal law is gradually developing in the direction of moderation [60]. Today, the development of AI technology has had a profound and far-reaching influence on virtually every aspect of our lives, from the way we work and communicate to how we access information and make decisions. AI has revolutionized industries such as healthcare, finance, and transportation, making processes more efficient and data-driven. As AI technology continues to advance, its influence will only become more pronounced, reshaping the future in ways both exciting and challenging [61, 119, 120].

Given this understanding, criminal law should minimize its interference in the development of AI when addressing AI-related crimes to facilitate a rational integration of criminal law with technological advancements. Essentially, this entails avoiding undue intrusion of criminal law in the realm of science and technology [37, 109]. Criminal law should remain adaptable and open to evolving regulations and legal frameworks. It must be capable of adjusting to emerging technologies and their potential legal implications. Therefore, criminal law should rationally intervene in the development of AI. This can be explained from the following aspects.

Firstly, criminal law should limit its regulatory scope. Criminal law, as protection law, is a secondary norm compared to other legal norms, and therefore its scope of regulation should be limited [121, 122]. In the course of its participation in social regulation, criminal law often interferes too much with social development because it fails to observe the boundaries with other laws and social norms. Indeed, the widespread issue of an overextension of national penal authority is a shared challenge encountered by nations in contemporary society [123]. The overzealous application of criminal law in the realm of social governance has led to a range of societal issues [124].

For instance, this overreach has altered the balance of state power and civil liberties, leading to an unwarranted amplification of the state's penal authority and an unjustified encroachment upon civil rights and freedoms. Furthermore, the excessive application of criminal law can lead to the inability of the state to rationally allocate its judicial resources, diminishing the state's capacity to prioritize the allocation of limited judicial resources for addressing general social disputes and legal violations [125, 126]. Finally, the overuse of criminal law will inevitably impede the economic and social innovation, resulting in the reduction of the incentive to innovate for the individuals who are severely restricted by the norms.

Therefore, for the development of AI, the rational intervention of the state should prioritize the establishment of industry norms and corresponding technical standards to lead to the development of AI technology. If the corresponding disputes occur in the application of AI, the state should give priority to repairing damaged social relations through the adjustment of civil norms. Ideally, criminal law should be allowed to intervene as a last resort, only when the aforementioned pre-existing norms, such as civil law and administrative law, have failed to provide a guarantee [123, 127, 128]. However, in the practice, for crimes involving AI, the choose of the relevant countermeasures completely ignores the positive role of pre-existing legal norms in the prevention and control of corresponding risks, and instead regards criminal law regulations as the only countermeasures. In the absence of clear provisions on the duty of care and distribution of responsibility in the development and application of AI technology, some opinions advocate direct intervention by criminal law, stipulating corresponding crimes, and establishing a corresponding penalty system [6, 129]. These are the manifestations of the transitional expansion of criminal law intervention. Especially the broad duty of care, as well as the strict liability provisions, these excessive interventions of the criminal law will seriously limit the innovation of AI researchers, designers, and producers, thus causing the development of AI technology to slow down or even stop [19, 130].

As a result, when responding to the challenges of AI, criminal law should still position themselves as protection law. Only when the purpose of regulation cannot be achieved after exhaustive adjustment of the antecedent legal norms, can the intervention of criminal law and the initiation of punishment be legitimate and reasonable, because only in this way can the excessive interference of criminal law in the field of science and technology be avoided [11, 131].

Secondly, criminal law should establish clear criteria for criminalization. The process of criminalization, or defining certain behaviors or actions as criminal offenses, is a complex and multifaceted one. The clear and identified criteria come into play when determining what should be criminalized within a legal system [132–134]. Generally speaking, criminal law norms define a specific act as a crime by describing its constituent elements. In order to realize the principle of the legality of crimes and penalties, the description of the constituent elements of a crime should be clear and unambiguous [135–137]. However, with the aim to cope with the risks posed by some specific behaviors, the legislator will adopt the legislative technique of general statement and great flexibility for the description of certain constituent elements. Only in this way can it be ensured that the coverage of criminal law norms is maximized, thus achieving the purpose of lowering the threshold of incrimination and expanding the application of criminal law in the practice. However, as a basic principle to protect the rights of criminals, the principle of legality of crime and punishment, requires the clarity and identification of criminal law norms so as to limit the arbitrary launch and expansion of the state's power of punishment [138, 139]. In this sense, the blurring of criminal law incrimination criteria objectively creates a lack of clarity in criminal law norms, thereby violating the basic principle of the legality of crimes and penalties.

In responding to the challenges posed by AI, some views, influenced by the instrumentalism of criminal law as a preferred way of managing society, continue to advocate the creation of underpinning provisions to maximize the inclusion of the crimes involving AI within the scope of normative regulation [140]. However, the excessive expansion of the scope of intervention of criminal law not only further erodes the human rights protection function of criminal law, but also promotes an unjustified and unlimited expansion of criminal law. Such normative expansion objectively provides a basis for the excessive expansion of criminal law in practice. As a result of this legislative model, criminal law has further strengthened its control over the technological sphere, which undoubtedly increases the risk that technological development and application will be hindered as a result of excessive interference by criminal law. In order to ensure the development and application of AI technology, it is important to protect the tendency of criminal law from expanding excessively into the field of technology. For the legislators, the criteria for criminalization must be clear and certain, so as to avoid the blurring of this criterion, which could result in the criminal law interfering excessively in the development and application of AI technology.

The conclusion that can be drawn from the above discussion is that criminal law should reasonably intervene in the development and application of AI technology. In response to the risks posed by crimes involving AI, criminal law should reasonably define the scope of its own intervention, so as to avoid its excessive interference by criminal law in the objects to which its norms are applied. In addition, legislators should ensure that the criteria of criminalization of AI is clear and unambiguous. Only in this way can the criminal law be prompted to abide by the boundaries of its own reasonable intervention in the technological risks, and to prevent the criminal law from unduly constraining technology, thereby ensuring that the development of science and technology is not impeded.

Modest and Restrictive Response to Crime Involving AI

In modern society, with the development and application of technology such as AI, the resulting technological risks have undoubtedly become a microcosm of the modern risk society [141, 142]. As the uncertainty of risk triggers public fear, the value of the defense function of criminal law is increasingly emphasized by society [143, 144]. These risks are often characterized by a high degree of uncertainty, which dictates that the response to them is primarily preventive. For the criminal law, this also determines the fact that criminal law countermeasures can intervene in advance. Specifically, the response of criminal law to some risks is no longer limited to the actual perpetrators, but regulates and adjusts the factors that create risks in advance, in order to achieve the preventive purpose of the criminal law. In this case, should the modest attributes of the criminal law give way to the need for prevention?

Of course, criminal law is designed to maintain order, protect individual rights, and punish those who violate the law. However, it is equally important for criminal law to be modest and restrictive in its application, ensuring that the legal system does not overstep its boundaries and respects the principles of justice [145, 146]. Therefore, the modest and restrictive attributes of criminal law are indispensable in maintaining a just and equitable legal system. By adhering to these principles, societies can strike a balance between maintaining order and safeguarding the liberties of all citizens, thereby upholding the core values of a democratic and lawful society. Specifically, how the criminal law maintains the balance between its modest and restrictive attributes and the crime prevention is a key to dealing with the risk of crimes involving AI. In our increasingly complex societies, there is a preference for criminal law to fulfill its preventive purpose without compromising its essential attribute of moderation and restriction [147]. In the practice, however, we have to choose a more important value as a foundation and base another value on the realization of the foundation value.

The moderation and restriction, as the essential attributes of criminal law, is not only related to the effective functioning of criminal law, but also maintains the rationality of criminal law itself. Although the preventive function of criminal law is of great significance in social development, it cannot be overemphasized in dealing with crimes involving AI. Therefore, crimes involving AI must be treated with caution on the basis of modesty and restriction in the criminal law, so as to avoid unnecessary preventive measures. This can be discussed in more detail from the following aspects.

Firstly, criminal law should adhere to its attribute of moderation and restriction in preventing crime. Like crime, punishment as a response to crime is equally an evil [148, 149]. Expansion and abuse in the application of criminal law should therefore be avoided. Thus, criminal law can only be used as a response to an infringement of a legal interest if other normative responses are ineffective. Criminal law thus has the character of a law of last resort. In modern societies, adherence to the attribute of the criminal law as a last resort must be accompanied by the moderation and restriction of the criminal law. Especially when dealing with the risks brought about by the development and application of AI, criminal law should maintain its attribute of moderation and restriction and avoid premature and excessive interference in this risk [109, 150]. Such risks posed by AI may or may not occur in reality, and if the criminal law interferes prematurely in these risks, it will unduly compress the space of freedom of citizens on the one hand, and impede the progress of technology on the other. Although the punishment is the most severe response, there is no evidence that this measure is the most appropriate means to deal with the risks of AI.

In essence, the moderation and restriction of criminal law requires that it be justified only when other means cannot play an effective role in responding to the risk. When dealing with the risks of AI, if the intervention of criminal law is first considered, other means of social governance will be abandoned and therefore unable to exert their governance effect. In the long run, this is not conducive to the effective prevention and control of social risks [151, 152]. In a society where AI poses increasing risks, criminal law cannot readily and limitlessly pre-emptively intervene in response to these risks by broadly categorizing behaviors as inherently dangerous in pursuit of its role in social defense. Indeed, doing so is essential to prevent criminal law from being reduced to a mere tool of social control and crime prevention.

Furthermore, the moderation and restriction of criminal law is reflected in criminal law legislation [124, 153]. The legislator may consider criminalizing an act only if the infringed legal interest cannot be protected by other laws and if the existing criminal law cannot reasonably deal with it at the same time [123]. Finally, the moderation and restriction of criminal law is equally reflected in the enforcement of penalties. If other legal norms can play a role in stopping aggression, removing obstacles, eliminating dangers, etc., then penalties cannot be used as a response to such risks.

Secondly, criminal law should rationally prevent crime. When dealing with the risks brought about by the development and application of AI, the rational criminal law response should be to avoid criminal law from overplaying its crime prevention function. Therefore, criminal law should strike a reasonable balance between its crime prevention function and its attributes of moderation and restriction. In this regard, some views have been expressed that, with the development and application of some new technology, it is reasonable that the corresponding risks have prompted criminal law to pay more attention to its preventive function [154, 155]. This can be proved by the newly amended criminal law that puts the protection of legal interests at the forefront and stipulates the large number of abstract dangerous offenders. Although this view is somewhat extreme, it also objectively reflects the trend, which the criminal law has weakened its moderation and restriction and strengthened its preventive function in dealing with the risk brought about the development and application of new technology.

Today, with the elevated risks associated with new technological development, the trend towards emphasizing the preventive function of criminal law should be viewed objectively. In fact, the creation of this value bias is in some sense justified. On the one hand, the social factual situation in which criminal law exists will naturally change the focus of criminal law on its functions. The theme of modern society no longer emphasizes, for example, how to avoid the excessive concentration of the state power or how to distribute freedom rationally, but rather how the State can act actively to guarantee the security [62, 82, 83]. On this premise, when people are confronted with risks in the society, there is an urgent need for the state to protect the security of social life through criminal law. Accordingly, such public opinions can often create the strong public pressure on the legislation of the criminal law, thus pushing the boundaries of criminal law defense forward [156, 157]. On the other hand, changes in the functions of government have likewise dictated a shift in the functioning of criminal law. In the traditional societies, citizens were more wary of the excessive government actions and its undue interference in the private sphere. However, in modern societies, citizens need the government to be able to effectively protest against the potential risks from political, economic and social sources. Therefore, providing citizens with a safe life has become the core mission of the government. Accordingly, as criminal law is an important means for the state to control society, the transformation of government tasks will naturally affect the position of its function [158].

Although it is reasonable for criminal law to emphasize its preventive function in dealing with the risks, which was brought about by the development and application of AI, this prevention must have certain limits and justifications. In this regard, some opinions advocate discussing the limits and reasons for the criminal law prevention from the following aspects: the effectiveness of its prevention, the types of legal interests infringed, and the consideration of the costs and expenses of the prevention [159, 160]. Although these views have different perspectives and emphases, they insist that the prevention of criminal law must be substantially restricted and have sufficient reasons [127, 161].

Adapting Theory to Deal with Crime Involving AI

In respond to the challenges to criminal imputation gaps posed by crimes involving AI, some have argued that a new system of criminal law theory should be reconstructed to provide a reasonable response from a theoretical point of view [117, 162].

However, according to the previous discussion, the criminal law norm and theory can still meet this challenge. In other words, the corresponding norm and theory have not been shaken in response to the challenge of stipulation for crimes involving AI. For this reason, it is reasonable to argue that the existing criminal law theory system should be adapted to meet the demands to respond to such gaps in the criminal imputation. This can be illustrated from the following aspects.

Firstly, the interpretative function of the criminal law norm should be fully utilized so as to increase the applicability of the norm in response to the imputation gaps. In practice, the rational application of criminal law provisions cannot be achieved without a scientific theory of norm interpretation [64, 163]. Accordingly, criminal law provisions are interpreted so as to enable a better normative evaluation of the fact and, ultimately, to resolve difficulties in the application of criminal law. Why can the interpretation of criminal law norms play a role in resolving this imputation gap? According to the conclusion of the previous discussion, the gap in the imputation for crimes involving AI exists only in the field of negligence crimes, and such gap has not impacted on the basis of the criminal law theoretical system, such as the subject of the crime, actus reus and responsibility. Therefore, with this fact that the criminal law norms and the traditional criminal theory can still be effectively applied in this kind of crime, the method of criminal law interpretation is completely sufficient to deal with this non-overall and non-fundamental gap in the imputation [19, 114].

Through the interpretation of criminal law norms, the difficulties in the application of criminal law norms are reduced, which objectively ensures the stability of criminal law norms to the utmost extent. Compared with reconstructing the theoretical system of criminal law, the interpretation is not to change the scope and the content of norms in its application, but to ensure the stability of norms on the premise of ensuring that the norms can be effectively applied [164, 165]. Today, although the crimes involving AI do bring certain risks to society, this highlights the importance of the stable value of the criminal law norms. For citizens, the stability of norms on the one hand ensures that he can guide his behavior according to the defined norms, on the other hand, it also ensures the stability of the boundaries of his own rights, thus maintaining his ability to resist the erosion of his rights by the public power. In addition, compared with large-scale emendation to the law, it is much more reasonable to deal with the gaps in the imputation for the negligence crime involving AI through the interpretation norms, because this can minimize the cost of responding to the challenges posed by the crimes involving AI [166].

Compared with directly reconstructing a new criminal law theoretical system, it is more direct and effective to deal with the gaps in the imputation for the crime involving AI through the normative interpretation, because the interpreted norms can be directly applied in practice. This interpretation is based on the existing legal norms, so the content of its interpretation will not go beyond the scope of the norms. As a method of applying legal norms, numerous interpretative conclusions can be drawn that can be directly used in practice. However, in order to deal with the gaps in the imputation for the crimes involving AI, a number of specific problems such as the abstraction of the foreseeable obligations and the breach of criminal liability are very common in such normative interpretations [37, 167]. Therefore, to deal with the gaps in the imputation for crimes involving AI through the normative explanations still requires an interpretive method that can bridge such gaps without endangering the entire system of criminal law.

Secondly, legislative responses to the gaps in the criminal imputation should be rationally limited. In response to the theoretical challenges posed by crimes involving AI, some opinions advocate that the gaps in criminal imputation should be filled through legislation on relevant facts of some crimes involving AI [168, 169]. However, such an endeavor raises a number of problems, and therefore such a proposition is not a reasonable response. Indeed, there should be rational limits to addressing the gap through legislation [170]. To some extent, legislation is undoubtedly the most direct and simple way to solve the problem in the practice. However, only when some certain crime phenomena that cannot be regulated by the existing criminal law and the corresponding legal interests that cannot be effectively protected do appear in society, such legislative response is necessary and rational [171, 172].

From an objective point of view, it is true that AI has already created many social risks and the gaps in the imputation for the negligence crimes involving AI. However, it is undeniable that crimes involving AI has not created new types of legal interests protected by criminal law, nor have they created the type of crimes that exceed the scope of existing criminal law norms. Therefore, on the premise that existing criminal law norms can still effectively regulate the current crimes involving AI, the attempts to deal with the related challenges through criminal legislation are indeed questionable [173]. If the criminal legislation is rashly passed to deal with such crimes, people will have reason to suspect that this is a symbolic legislation. This kind of symbolic legislation is mainly to appease the widespread concerns in society about the risk caused by the development and application of AI technology, and is also to strengthen social control through such criminal legislation [174–176]. However, such legislation undoubtedly creates the danger of instrumentalization of the criminal law, but also the unreasonable expansion of penal power and the squeezing of civil rights space.

2.3.3 Practical Requirements to Deal with the Imputation Gaps

Excluding AI as the subject of a crime and the necessity to maintain the stability of the theoretical framework of criminal law have presented challenges in addressing the gaps in the imputation for negligence crimes involving AI. Nevertheless, in practice, given the widespread use of AI technology, there is also a pressing need to sensibly address these imputation gaps. Therefore, under the premise of avoiding destabilizing the criminal law theoretical system, weakening the criminal liability and shaking the foundation of punishment, how to effectively solve the gaps in the imputation for the crimes involving AI is the purpose of the criminal law to cope with this theoretical problem, as well as the practical need to cope with this problem. This can be discussed in the following aspects.

Objectively speaking, it is precisely because the construction of the traditional negligence crime theory is difficult to make a normatively reasonable evaluation of the technical characteristics of AI, which results in the creation of the imputation gaps when attributing responsibility for negligence crimes involving AI [18, 59, 177]. Therefore, how to reasonably bridge such imputation gaps is a realistic choice for the criminal law to deal with this attribution dilemma. To this end, efforts need to be made in the following areas: first, the foreseeability in the context of negligence crimes should be reasonably understood. Theoretically, foreseeability of the perpetrator is the prerequisite for the imputation for the negligence crimes [153, 178, 179]. For him, the consequences caused by his actions can only be attributed to him if he has the foreseeable possibility of the consequences. However, in the negligence crimes involving AI, the perpetrator has no possibility to foresee the consequences of his actions. This is the main impact of AI technology on the negligence crime [20, 180]. It is precisely because of this impact that the issue of the gap in the imputation for the negligence crimes involving AI has arisen. Therefore, in order to reasonably attribute the result to the perpetrator, the imputation theory must necessarily overcome the attribution dilemma posed by the perpetrator's inability to foresee in order to deal with the imputation dilemma of crimes involving AI.

Secondly, according to the prevailing theoretical understanding of negligence crime, the perpetrator should have a general foresight of the causal flow of the result triggered by his behavior. However, in the negligence crimes involving AI, it is very difficult to determine such causal flow between the behavior and the result. Therefore, in order to solve this imputation gap problem, the causal flow needs to be rethought from a rational perspective. Whether this specific causal flow should be considered at the factual level or the normative level has become an important issue faced by criminal law in dealing with the gaps in imputation for the negligence crimes involving AI [181, 182]. In the negligence crimes involving AI, if the issue of causation is considered purely on the factual level, there is no way to objectively determine the causal flow.

Therefore, how to evaluate this specific causation from a normative level is a key to solving the problem of imputation gap. In addition, as more and more scholars are in favor of considering the violation of duty of care as an objective constituent element of the negligence crime, its judgment relies much more on the supplementation of other norms in practice [183–185]. In the negligence crime involving AI, the content of other norms is decisive for the judgment of the violation of such duty. However, since the development of AI is still in its primary stage, the relevant laws and regulations on AI have not yet been established, and normative documents such as relevant guidelines and professional standards for AI are still lacking in perfection [186–188]. Under this premise, on the one hand, the establishment of relevant laws and regulations and professional standards should be accelerated, and on the other hand, it is still necessary to make up for the lack of norms in the judgment of the duty of care through the understanding of criminal law.

Moreover, in the negligence crimes involving AI, how to rationally allocate the duty of care among different subjects similarly affects the attribution of responsibility among different subjects. In the traditional attribution of negligence crimes, the correspondence between subject-object is more often emphasized [183, 189]. However, in the development and application of AI technology, the process of production, design and manufacture of AI is divided into numerous stages as the degree of specialization of AI technology and the production process are more finely delineated. Accordingly, the corresponding participants in different stages may only have some control within the stage they are in, and therefore beyond the stage they are in will not have the possibility of foresight.

In this case, participants in the different stages may only have certain control capabilities within the stage they are in, so they will have no possibility to foresee beyond the stage they are in [117, 190]. In the context of an increasingly sophisticated division of labor in AI products, the relationship between participants plays a crucial role in the rational allocation of corresponding responsibilities. This is driven by the coherence of technology and the production process, which is often a result of a specific outcome occurring in multiple links or processes.

The analysis of the theoretical premises of imputation for the negligence crimes involving AI in this chapter reveals that the response to the imputation gaps should first exclude the possibility of AI as the subject of the crime. This is because AI should not be the subject of a crime, either from the normative perspective or from the factual perspective. Moreover, the existing normative system of criminal law, which is based on the natural person, can still cope with the specificity of the subject of crime involving AI. With regard to the criminal response to such imputation gaps, the criminal law should adhere to its modest and restrictive attributes in the practice.

References

1. Holzinger A, Keiblinger K, Holub P, Zatloukal K, Müller H (2023) AI for life: Trends in artificial intelligence for biotechnology. New Biotechnol 74:16–24. https://doi.org/10.1016/j.nbt.2023.02.001
2. Makridakis S (2017) The forthcoming artificial intelligence (AI) revolution: its impact on society and firms. Futures 90:46–60. https://doi.org/10.1016/j.futures.2017.03.006
3. Stone P, Brooks R, Brynjolfsson E, Calo R, Etzioni O, Hager G et al (2022) Artificial intelligence and life in 2030: the one hundred year study on artificial intelligence. arXiv preprint arXiv:2211.06318. https://doi.org/10.48550/arXiv.2211.06318
4. Dremliuga R, Prisekina N (2020) The concept of culpability in criminal law and AI systems. J Polit Law 13(3):256. https://doi.org/10.5539/jpl.v13n3p256
5. Yeoh P (2019) Artificial intelligence: accelerator or panacea for financial crime? J Finan Crime 26(2):634–646. https://doi.org/10.1108/JFC-08-2018-0077
6. Lima D (2017) Could AI agents be held criminally liable: artificial intelligence and the challenges for criminal law. SCL Rev 69:677
7. Vuletić I (2021) Criminal law and the challenges of autonomous intelligence: substituting a theory of guilt with the division of labor. In: The law and economics of patent damages, antitrust, and legal process. Emerald Publishing Limited, pp 111–126. https://doi.org/10.1108/S0193-589520210000029007
8. Dobrinoiu M (2019) The influence of artificial intelligence on criminal liability. LESIJ-Lex ET Sci Int J 26(1):140–147

9. Hallevy G (2015) Liability for crimes involving artificial intelligence systems, vol 257. Springer, New York. https://doi.org/10.1007/978-3-319-10124-8
10. Canter D (2000) Offender profiling and criminal differentiation. Legal Criminol Psychol 5(1):23–46. https://doi.org/10.1348/135532500167958
11. Caldwell M, Andrews JT, Tanay T, Griffin LD (2020) AI-enabled future crime. Crime Sci 9(1):1–13. https://doi.org/10.1186/s40163-020-00123-8
12. Jeong D (2020) Artificial intelligence security threat, crime, and forensics: taxonomy and open issues. IEEE Access 8:184560–184574. https://doi.org/10.1109/ACCESS.2020.3029280
13. Brown DK (2012) Criminal law reform and the persistence of strict liability. Duke Law J 62(2):285–338
14. Maddox JR (1985) Products liability in Europe: towards a regime of strict liability. J World Trade L 19:508
15. Schneebaum SM (1989) Products liability in the European community: what does it mean for US companies? Food Drug Cosmet Law J 44(3):283–289
16. Carpenter CL (2003) On statutory rape, strict liability, and the public welfare offense model. Am UL Rev 53:313
17. Iguh NA, Oti-Onyema LA (2020) Statutory rape under the child's right act of Nigeria: analysis of the criminal responsibility of a child offender. IJOCLLEP 2:184
18. Bashayreh M, Sibai FN, Tabbara A (2021) Artificial intelligence and legal liability: towards an international approach of proportional liability based on risk sharing. Inform Commun Technol Law 30(2):169–192. https://doi.org/10.1080/13600834.2020.1856025
19. King TC, Aggarwal N, Taddeo M, Floridi L (2020) Artificial intelligence crime: an interdisciplinary analysis of foreseeable threats and solutions. Sci Eng Ethics 26:89–120. https://doi.org/10.1007/s11948-018-00081-0
20. Kingston JK (2016) Artificial intelligence and legal liability. Artificial intelligence and legal liability. In: Bramer M, Petridis M (eds) Research and development in intelligent systems XXXIII. SGAI 2016. Springer, Cham. https://doi.org/10.1007/978-3-319-47175-4_20
21. Spindler G (2019) User liability and strict liability in the Internet of Things and for robots. In: Liability for artificial intelligence and the internet of things. Nomos Verlagsgesellschaft mbH & Co. KG, pp 125–144. https://doi.org/10.5771/9783845294797
22. Wendehorst C (2020) Strict liability for AI and other emerging technologies. J Eur Tort Law 11(2):150–180. https://doi.org/10.1515/jetl-2020-0140
23. Csitei B (2020) Self-driving cars and criminal liability. Debreceni Jogi Muhely, p 34
24. Gless S, Silverman E, Weigend T (2016) If robots cause harm, who is to blame? Self-driving cars and criminal liability. New Crim Law Rev 19(3):412–436. https://doi.org/10.1525/nclr.2016.19.3.412
25. Lohmann MF (2016) Liability issues concerning self-driving vehicles. Eur J Risk Regul 7(2):335–340. https://doi.org/10.1017/S1867299X00005754
26. Feiler J (2023) The artificially intelligent trolley problem: understanding our criminal law gaps in a robot driven world. Hastings Sci Tech LJ 14:1
27. Günsberg PS (2022) Automated vehicles: is a dilution of human responsibility the answer? New J Eur Crim Law 13(4):439–451. https://doi.org/10.1177/20322844221113804
28. Justo-Hanani R (2022) The politics of artificial intelligence regulation and governance reform in the European Union. Policy Sci 55(1):137–159. https://doi.org/10.1007/s11077-022-09452-8
29. Veale M, Zuiderveen Borgesius F (2021) Demystifying the draft EU artificial intelligence act—analysing the good, the bad, and the unclear elements of the proposed approach. Comput Law Rev Int 22(4), 97-112. https://doi.org/10.9785/cri-2021-220402
30. Khan KF, Ali A, Khan ZF, Siddiqua H (2021) Artificial intelligence and criminal culpability. In: Proceedings of the 2021 international conference on innovative computing (ICIC). IEEE, pp 1–7. https://doi.org/10.1109/ICIC53490.2021.9692954

31. Rachum-Twaig O, Somech O (2022) The law of AI: a renegotiation or a reproduction commentary on Ryan Abbott, the reasonable robot. Jerus Rev Legal Stud 25(1):1–17. https://doi.org/10.1093/jrls/jlac002
32. Han J, Huang Y, Liu S, Towey K (2020) Artificial intelligence for anti-money laundering: a review and extension. Dig Finance 2(3–4):211–239. https://doi.org/10.1007/s42521-020-00023-1
33. Van den Hoven van Genderen R (2018) Do we need new legal personhood in the age of robots and AI? In: Robotics, AI and the future of law. Springer, Singapore, pp 15–55. https://doi.org/10.1007/978-981-13-2874-9_2
34. Abbott R, Sarch A (2019) Punishing artificial intelligence: legal fiction or science fiction. UC Davis Law Rev 53:323. https://doi.org/10.2139/ssrn.3327485
35. Gaifutdinov RG, Begishev IR, Khisamova ZI, Sidorenko EL, Bersei DD, Musina RR (2021) Conceptual bases of criminal punishment application regarding artificial intelligence. Rev San Greg 44:211–216
36. Brundage M, Avin S, Clark J, Toner H, Eckersley P, Garfinkel B et al (2018) The malicious use of artificial intelligence: forecasting, prevention, and mitigation
37. Lagioia F, Sartor G (2020) AI systems under criminal law: a legal analysis and a regulatory perspective. Philos Technol 33(3):433–465. https://doi.org/10.1007/s13347-019-00362-x
38. Bianchi F, Curry AC, Hovy D (2023) Artificial intelligence accidents waiting to happen? J Artif Intell Res 76:193–199. https://doi.org/10.1613/jair.1.14263
39. Wei M, Zhou Z (2022) AI ethics issues in real world: evidence from AI incident database. arXiv preprint arXiv:2206.07635. https://doi.org/10.48550/arXiv.2206.07635
40. Reed C (2018) How should we regulate artificial intelligence? Philos Trans R Soc A Math Phys Eng Sci 376(2128):20170360. https://doi.org/10.1098/rsta.2017.0360
41. Sullivan HR, Schweikart SJ (2019) Are current tort liability doctrines adequate for addressing injury caused by AI? AMA J Ethics 21(2):160–166. https://doi.org/10.1001/amajethics.2019.160
42. Wasserstrom RA (2017) Strict liability in the criminal law. The structure and limits of criminal law. Routledge, New York, pp 395–410
43. Freitas PM, Andrade F, Novais P (2014) Criminal liability of autonomous agents: from the unthinkable to the plausible. In: Casanovas P, Pagallo U, Palmirani M, Sartor G (eds) AI approaches to the complexity of legal systems. AICOL 2013. Lecture notes in computer science, vol 8929. Springer, Berlin. https://doi.org/10.1007/978-3-662-45960-7_11
44. Cunneen M, Mullins M, Murphy F (2020) Artificial intelligence assistants and risk: framing a connectivity risk narrative. AI Soc 35:625–634. https://doi.org/10.1007/s00146-019-00916-9
45. Floridi L, Cowls J, Beltrametti M, Chatila R, Chazerand P, Dignum V et al (2021) An ethical framework for a good AI society: opportunities, risks, principles, and recommendations. Ethics Govern Polic Artif Intell 12:19–39. https://doi.org/10.1007/978-3-030-81907-1_3
46. Osoba OA, Welser W (2017) The risks of artificial intelligence to security and the future of work. RAND, Santa Monica
47. Broadhurst R, Maxim D, Brown P, Trivedi H, Wang J (2019) Artificial intelligence and crime. Available at SSRN 3407779. https://doi.org/10.2139/ssrn.3407779
48. Blauth TF, Gstrein OJ, Zwitter A (2022) Artificial intelligence crime: an overview of malicious use and abuse of AI. IEEE Access 10:77110–77122. https://doi.org/10.1109/ACCESS.2022.3191790
49. Mosechkin IN (2019) Artificial intelligence and criminal liability: problems of becoming a new type of crime subject. Vestnik Saint Petersburg UL, p 461. https://doi.org/10.21608/ihites.2021.90657.1049
50. Hallevy G (2013) When robots kill: artificial intelligence under criminal law. UPNE
51. Moore MS (2010) Act and crime: the philosophy of action and its implications for criminal law. Oxford University Press, Oxford

52. Robinson PH (1993) Should the criminal law abandon the actus reus-mens rea distinction? In: Shute S, Gardner J, Horder J (eds) Criminal law: action, value and structure. Oxford University Press, Oxford, pp 187–211. https://ssrn.com/abstract=661202
53. Huang H (2020) Analysis on the criminal subject of artificial intelligence. In: Data processing techniques and applications for cyber-physical systems (DPTA 2019). Springer, Singapore, pp 317–321. https://doi.org/10.1007/978-981-15-1468-5_40
54. Kirpichnikov D, Pavlyuk A, Grebneva Y, Okagbue H (2020) Criminal liability of the artificial intelligence. In: E3S web of conferences, vol 159. EDP Sciences, p 04025
55. Gruodytė E, Čerka P (2020) Artificial intelligence as a subject of criminal law: a corporate liability model perspective. In: Smart technologies and fundamental rights. Brill, pp 260–281. https://doi.org/10.1163/9789004437876_013
56. Hallevy G (2010) I, Robot-I, criminal: when science fiction becomes reality: legal liability of AI robots committing criminal offenses. Syracuse Sci Technol Law Rep 1:1442
57. Das AK, Ashrafi A, Ahmmad M (2019) Joint cognition of both human and machine for predicting criminal punishment in judicial system. In: Proceedings of the 2019 IEEE 4th international conference on computer and communication systems (ICCCS). IEEE, pp 36–40. https://doi.org/10.1109/CCOMS.2019.8821655
58. Rossmy B, Völkel ST, Naphausen E, Kimm P, Wiethoff A, Muxel A (2020) Punishable AI: examining users' attitude towards robot punishment. In: Proceedings of the 2020 ACM designing interactive systems conference, pp 179–191. https://doi.org/10.1145/3357236.3395542
59. Giannini A, Kwik J (2023) Negligence failures and negligence fixes. A comparative analysis of criminal regulation of AI and autonomous vehicles. In: Criminal law forum. Springer, Dordrecht, pp 1–43. https://doi.org/10.1007/s10609-023-09451-1
60. Duff RA (2013) Towards a modest legal moralism. Crim Law Philos 8:12–28
61. Goralski MA, Tan TK (2020) Artificial intelligence and sustainable development. Int J Manag Educ 18(1):100330. https://doi.org/10.1016/j.ijme.2019.100330
62. Levin B (2022) Criminal law exceptionalism. Va L Rev 108:1381. https://doi.org/10.2139/ssrn.4098101
63. Bertolini A, Episcopo F (2022) Robots and AI as legal subjects? Disentangling the ontological and functional perspective. Front Robot AI 9:842213. https://doi.org/10.3389/frobt.2022.842213
64. Maculan E, Gil Gil A (2020) The rationale and purposes of criminal law and punishment in transitional contexts. Oxford J Legal Stud 40(1):132–157. https://doi.org/10.1093/ojls/gqz033
65. Simmler M, Markwalder N (2019) Guilty robots? Rethinking the nature of culpability and legal personhood in an age of artificial intelligence. In: Criminal law forum, vol 30. Springer, New York, pp 1–31. https://doi.org/10.1007/s10609-018-9360-0
66. Duff RA (1993) Choice, character, and criminal liability. Law Philos 12:345
67. Weissman A, Weissman A (2007) Rethinking criminal corporate liability. Ind L J 82:411
68. Zech H (2021) Liability for AI: public policy considerations. In: ERA forum, vol 22. Springer, Berlin, pp 147–158. https://doi.org/10.1007/s12027-020-00648-0
69. Bayles MD (1982) Character, purpose, and criminal responsibility. Law Philos 1(1):5–20
70. Chesterman S (2020) Artificial intelligence and the limits of legal personality. Int Comp Law Quart 69(4):819–844. https://doi.org/10.1017/S0020589320000366
71. Morse SJ (2006) Criminal responsibility and the disappearing person. Cardozo L Rev 28:2545
72. Begishev IR, Kirillov MA, Bersei DD, Nechaeva EV, Perepelkin VI, Serkova TV et al (2023) Robotics, artificial intelligence and criminal law: an overview of contemporary studies. In: AIP conference proceedings, vol 2701. AIP Publishing LLC, p 020033. https://doi.org/10.1063/5.0130210
73. Bikeev I, Kabanov P, Begishev I, Khisamova Z (2019) Criminological risks and legal aspects of artificial intelligence implementation. In: Proceedings of the international conference on artificial intelligence, information processing and cloud computing, pp 1–7. https://doi.org/10.1145/3371425.3371476

74. Archer MS (2021) Friendship between human beings and AI robots? In: Robotics, AI, and humanity: science, ethics, and policy, pp 177–189. https://doi.org/10.1007/978-3-030-54173-6_15
75. Gopnik A (2017) Making AI more human. Sci Am 316(6):60–65
76. Olivier B (2017) Artificial intelligence (AI) and being human: what is the difference? Acta Acad Crit Views Soc Cult Polit 49(1):2–21
77. Pelau C, Dabija DC, Ene I (2021) What makes an AI device human-like? The role of interaction quality, empathy and perceived psychological anthropomorphic characteristics in the acceptance of artificial intelligence in the service industry. Comput Hum Behav 122:106855. https://doi.org/10.1016/j.chb.2021.106855
78. Lacey N (2016) In search of criminal responsibility: ideas, interests, and institutions. Oxford University Press, Oxford
79. Packer IK (2009) Evaluation of criminal responsibility. Oxford University Press, Oxford
80. Alper JS (1998) Genes, free will, and criminal responsibility. Soc Sci Med 46(12):1599–1611. https://doi.org/10.1016/S0277-9536(97)10136-8
81. Kenny A (2011) Freewill and responsibility (Routledge revivals). Routledge, New York
82. Lacey N (2001) In search of the responsible subject: history, philosophy and social sciences in criminal law theory. Mod Law Rev 64(3):350–371. https://doi.org/10.1111/1468-2230.00325
83. Lacey N (2001) Responsibility and modernity in criminal law. J Polit Philos 9(3):249–276. https://doi.org/10.1111/1467-9760.00127
84. O'Connor T (2000) Causality, mind, and free will. Philos Perspect 14:105–117
85. Williams G (2023) Anomalous mind-matter influence, free will, and the nature of causality. J Anomal Exp Cognit 3(1):140–173
86. Singer W, Topp S (2023) Neuroscience history interview with Professor Wolf Singer, emeritus director at the Department of Neurophysiology, Max Planck Institute for brain research in Frankfurt am main. J Hist Neurosci 32(2):148–172. https://doi.org/10.1080/0964704X.2021.1904714
87. Singer W (2017) Freiheitserfahrung als soziale Realität? In: Freiheit. Begründung und Entfaltung in philosophie, religion und kultur. Vandenhoeck & Ruprecht GmbH & Co. KG, pp 125–138
88. Habermas J (2007) The language game of responsible agency and the problem of free will: how can epistemic dualism be reconciled with ontological monism? Philos Explor 10(1):13–50. https://doi.org/10.1080/13869790601170128
89. Moyar D, Walsh KP, Rand S (eds) (2022) Hegel's philosophy of right: critical perspectives on freedom and history. Taylor & Francis
90. Gladden M, Fortuna P, Modliński A (2022) The empowerment of artificial intelligence in post-digital organizations: exploring human interactions with supervisory AI. Hum Technol 18(2):98–121
91. Kumar R, Gupta P, Singh S, Jain D (2021) Human empowerment by Industry 5.0 in digital era: analysis of enablers. In: Advances in industrial and production engineering: select proceedings of FLAME 2020. Springer, Singapore, pp 401–410. https://doi.org/10.1007/978-981-33-4320-7_36
92. Craigie J (2015) Against a singular understanding of legal capacity: criminal responsibility and the convention on the rights of persons with disabilities. Int J Law Psych 40:6–14. https://doi.org/10.1016/j.ijlp.2015.04.002
93. Brandtzaeg PB, Skjuve M, Følstad A (2022) My AI friend: how users of a social chatbot understand their human–AI friendship. Hum Commun Res 48(3):404–429. https://doi.org/10.1093/hcr/hqac008
94. Codoban AT (2020) Why can't AI understand images as man does? Postmod Open 11(4):174–182
95. Dobrev D (2018) How does the AI understand what's going on. arXiv preprint arXiv:1805.00851. https://doi.org/10.48550/arXiv.1805.00851

96. Elayan H, Aloqaily M, Karray F, Guizani M (2022) Internet of behavior (IOB) and explainable AI systems for influencing IoT behavior. IEEE Netw. https://doi.org/10.1109/MNET.009.2100500
97. Mäntymäki M, Minkkinen M, Birkstedt T, Viljanen M (2022) Defining organizational AI governance. AI Ethics 2(4):603–609. https://doi.org/10.1007/s43681-022-00143-x
98. Kosuru VSR, Venkitaraman AK (2023) Advancements and challenges in achieving fully autonomous self-driving vehicles. World J Adv Res Rev 18(1):161–167
99. Russell S (2019) Human compatible: artificial intelligence and the problem of control. Penguin
100. Swanepoel D (2021) The possibility of deliberate norm-adherence in AI. Ethics Inform Technol 23(2):157–163. https://doi.org/10.1007/s10676-020-09535-1
101. Mathias CW, Marsh-Richard DM, Dougherty DM (2008) Behavioral measures of impulsivity and the law. Behav Sci Law 26(6):691–707. https://doi.org/10.1002/bsl.841
102. Chowdhury S, Dey P, Joel-Edgar S, Bhattacharya S, Rodriguez-Espindola O, Abadie A, Truong L (2023) Unlocking the value of artificial intelligence in human resource management through AI capability framework. Hum Resour Manag Rev 33(1):100899. https://doi.org/10.1016/j.hrmr.2022.100899
103. Zhang H, Song M, Wang Y (2023) Does AI-infused operations capability enhance or impede the relationship between information technology capability and firm performance? Technol Forecast Soc Change 191:122517. https://doi.org/10.1016/j.techfore.2023.122517
104. Goyal A, Bengio Y (2022) Inductive biases for deep learning of higher-level cognition. Proceed R Soc A 478(2266):20210068. https://doi.org/10.1098/rspa.2021.0068
105. Helbing D (2019) Societal, economic, ethical and legal challenges of the digital revolution: from big data to deep learning, artificial intelligence, and manipulative technologies. Springer, New York, pp 47–72. https://doi.org/10.1007/978-3-319-90869-4_6
106. Kolber AJ (2009) The subjective experience of punishment. Columbia Law Rev 40:182–236
107. Dubber MD (1996) The pain of punishment. Buff Law Rev 44:545
108. Shoemaker K (2001) The problem of pain in punishment: historical perspectives. In: Pain, death, and the law, pp 15–41
109. Custers B (2022) AI in criminal law: an overview of AI applications in substantive and procedural criminal law. In: Law and artificial intelligence: regulating AI and applying AI in legal practice, pp 205–223. https://doi.org/10.1007/978-94-6265-523-2_11
110. Barabas C (2020) Beyond bias: re-imagining the terms of "ethical AI" in criminal law. Geol J Law Mod Crit Race Persp 12:83. https://doi.org/10.2139/ssrn.3377921
111. Sukhodolov AP, Bychkov AV, Bychkova AM (2020) Criminal policy for crimes committed using artificial intelligence technologies: state, problems, prospects. https://doi.org/10.17516/1997-1370-0542
112. Au-Yong-Oliveira M, Canastro D, Oliveira J, Tomás J, Amorim S, Moreira F (2019) The role of AI and automation on the future of jobs and the opportunity to change society. In: New knowledge in information systems and technologies, vol 3. Springer, New York, pp 348–357. https://doi.org/10.1007/978-3-030-16187-3_34
113. Wamba SF, Bawack RE, Guthrie C, Queiroz MM, Carillo KDA (2021) Are we preparing for a good AI society? A bibliometric review and research agenda. Technol Forecast Soc Change 164:120482. https://doi.org/10.1016/j.techfore.2020.120482
114. Ahmad MA, Eckert C, Teredesai A (2019) The challenge of imputation in explainable artificial intelligence models. arXiv preprint arXiv:1907.12669. https://doi.org/10.48550/arXiv.1907.12669
115. Caton S, Malisetty S, Haas C (2022) Impact of imputation strategies on fairness in machine learning. J Artif Intell Res 74:1011–1035. https://doi.org/10.1613/jair.1.13197
116. Kingston JK (2016) Artificial intelligence and legal liability. In: Research and development in intelligent systems XXXIII: incorporating applications and innovations in intelligent systems XXIV 33. Springer, New York, pp 269–279. https://doi.org/10.1007/978-3-319-47175-4_20
117. Osmani N (2020) The complexity of criminal liability of AI systems. Masaryk Univ J Law Technol 14(1):53–82. https://doi.org/10.5817/MUJLT2020-1-3

118. Selbst AD (2020) Negligence and AI's human users. BUL Rev 100:1315
119. Lee KF, Qiufan C (2021) AI 2041: ten visions for our future. Crown Currency
120. Wilks YA (2023) Artificial intelligence: modern magic or dangerous future? MIT Press
121. Bowles R, Faure M, Garoupa N (2008) The scope of criminal law and criminal sanctions: an economic view and policy implications. J Law Soc 35(3):389–416. https://doi.org/10.1111/j.1467-6478.2008.00444.x
122. Lacey N (2004) Criminalisation as regulation: the role of criminal law. Regul Law, pp 144–167. https://doi.org/10.2139/ssrn.2126521
123. Husak D (2008) Overcriminalization: the limits of the criminal law. Oxford University Press, Oxford
124. Ashworth A (2007) Conceptions of over criminalization. Ohio St J Crim Law 5:407–425
125. Benson BL, Kim I (2014) Causes and consequences of over-criminalization. Dept. of Economics Working Paper, SungKyunKwan University
126. Kim D, Kim I (2015) Trade-offs in the allocation of prosecution resources: an opportunity cost of over criminalization. Appl Econ 47(16):1652–1669. https://doi.org/10.1080/00036846.2014.1000531
127. Husak D (2004) The criminal law as last resort. Oxford J Legal Stud 24(2):207–235. https://doi.org/10.1093/ojls/24.2.207
128. Jareborg N (2004) Criminalization as last resort (Ultima Ratio). Ohio St J Crim Law 2:521
129. Yew RJ, Hadfield-Menell D (2022) A penalty default approach to preemptive harm disclosure and mitigation for AI systems. In: Proceedings of the 2022 AAAI/ACM conference on AI, ethics, and society, pp 823–830. https://doi.org/10.1145/3514094.3534130
130. Liu HY, Maas M, Danaher J, Scarcella L, Lexer M, Van Rompaey L (2020) Artificial intelligence and legal disruption: a new model for analysis. Law Innov Technol 12(2):205–258. https://doi.org/10.1080/17579961.2020.1815402
131. Greenstein S (2022) Preserving the rule of law in the era of artificial intelligence (AI). Artif Intell Law 30(3):291–323. https://doi.org/10.1007/s10506-021-09294-4
132. Harduf A (2013) How crimes should be created: a practical theory of criminalization. Crim Law Bull 49(1):325
133. Petersen S (2020) Why criminalize? Springer, New York
134. Svatikova K (2009) Economic criteria for criminalization: why do we need the criminal law? https://doi.org/10.2139/ssrn.1150689
135. Dana S (2008) Beyond retroactivity to realizing justice: a theory on the principle of legality in international criminal law sentencing. J Crim Law Criminol 99:857
136. Jordaan L, Terblanche SS (2012) Does the principle of legality require statutory crimes to have specific penalty clauses? A critical analysis of the decisions of the High Court and the Supreme Court of Appeal in DPP, Western Cape v Prins: comments. South Afr J Crim Just 25(3):379–389
137. Mitsilegas V, Billis E (2022) Article 49: principles of legality and proportionality of criminal offences and penalties. In: The EU charter of fundamental rights. Nomos Verlagsgesellschaft mbH & Co. KG, pp 1473–1508
138. Gottschalk M (2013) The Carceral state and the politics of punishment. In: The Sage handbook of punishment and society, pp 205–241
139. Ristroph A (2007) State intentions and the law of punishment. J Crim Law Criminol 98:1353
140. Mahmud A (2023) Application and criminalization of artificial intelligence in the digital society: security threats and the regulatory challenges. J Appl Sec Res 18(1):1–15. https://doi.org/10.1080/19361610.2021.1947113
141. Shimizu ML, Clark A, Shimizu M, Clark A (2019) Advanced technologies in a modern risk society: role of resilience-based approaches and public policy. Nexus Resil Publ Policy Mod Risk Soc 10:127–136. https://doi.org/10.1007/978-981-10-7362-5_8
142. Sørensen M, Christiansen A (2012) Ulrich beck: an introduction to the theory of second modernity and the risk society. Routledge, New York

143. Hudson B (2012) Punishment, rights and difference: defending justice in the risk society. In: Crime, risk and justice. Willan, pp 144–172
144. O'Malley PAT (2002) Risk societies and the government of crime. In: Dangerous offenders. Routledge, pp 27–44
145. Barnum TC, Nagin D (2023) Deterrence and sanction certainty perceptions. In: Oxford research encyclopedia of criminology and criminal justice. https://doi.org/10.1093/acrefore/9780190264079.013.248
146. Meyer F (2023) 19 Rethinking European criminal law. In: The Cambridge companion to European criminal law, p 461
147. Burzinji ZAQ, Yusoff WS, Rosbi MSBM, Salleh MFM, Abdullah AH (2022) The effect of forensic accounting on fraud prevention, the moderating role internal control effectiveness. Int J Econ Commer Manag 10(1):213–230
148. Lopes E (2022) Punishment for the failed criminal. Ephem Undergrad J Philos 22(1):2
149. Meyers C (2022) Crime and punishment. In: Drug legalization: a philosophical analysis. Springer, Cham, pp 181–201. https://doi.org/10.1007/978-3-031-17005-8_9
150. Ivan DL, Manea T (2022) AI use in criminal matters as permitted under EU law and as needed to safeguard the essence of fundamental rights. Int J Law Chang World 1(1):17–32
151. Pratt J, Miao M (2019) Risk, populism, and criminal law. New Crim Law Rev 22(4):391–433. https://doi.org/10.1525/nclr.2019.22.4.391
152. Slobogin C (2005) The civilization of the criminal law. Vand L Rev 58:121
153. Hall J (2010) General principles of criminal law. The Lawbook Exchange, Ltd
154. Albrecht HJ, Kilchling M (2002) Crime risk assessment, legislation, and the prevention of serious crime-comparative perspectives. Eur J Crime Crim Law Crim Just 10:23. https://doi.org/10.1163/15718170220519515
155. Lomell HM (2012) Punishing the uncommitted crime: prevention, pre-emption, precaution and the transformation of criminal law. In: Justice and security in the 21st century. Routledge, pp 83–100
156. de Carvalho VDH, Costa APCS (2022) Towards corpora creation from social web in Brazilian Portuguese to support public security analyses and decisions. Library Hi Tech. https://doi.org/10.1108/LHT-08-2022-0401
157. Martín N (2022) Global criminal law. Springer, New York
158. Wells H (2022) The fast and the furious: drivers, speed cameras and control in a risk society. CRC Press. https://doi.org/10.4324/9781315558219
159. Brown DK (2004) Cost-benefit analysis in criminal law. California Law Rev 12:323–372. https://doi.org/10.2307/3481427
160. Welsh BC, Farrington DP, Gowar BR (2015) Benefit-cost analysis of crime prevention programs. Crime Just 44(1):447–516. https://doi.org/10.1007/s10610-022-09527-5
161. Cheh MM (1990) Constitutional limits on using civil remedies to achieve criminal law objectives: understanding and transcending the criminal-civil law distinction. Hastings LJ 42:1325
162. Stanila L (2020) Living in the future: new actors in the field of criminal law—artificial intelligence. In: Legal science: functions, significance and future in legal systems II, p 300. https://doi.org/10.22364/iscflul.7.2.24
163. Hessick CB, Kennedy JE (2019) Criminal clear statement rules. Wash Univ Law Rev 97:351
164. Funk P (2005) Governmental action, social norms, and criminal behavior. J Instit Theor Econ Zeitschrift für die gesamte Staatswissenschaft 40:522–535
165. Simmler M (2020) The importance of placing blame: criminal law and the stabilization of norms. In: Criminal law forum, vol 31. Springer, New York, pp 147–178. https://doi.org/10.1007/s10609-020-09390-1
166. Shillito MR (2019) Untangling the 'dark web': an emerging technological challenge for the criminal law. Inform Commun Technol Law 28(2):186–207. https://doi.org/10.1080/13600834.2019.1623449

167. Kelman M (1981) Interpretive construction in the substantive criminal law. Stanf Law Rev 30:591–673. https://doi.org/10.2307/1228535
168. de Matos Pinto I (2021) The draft AI Act: a success story of strengthening Parliament's right of legislative initiative? In: ERA forum, vol 22. Springer, Berlin, pp 619–641. https://doi.org/10.1007/s12027-021-00691-5
169. Hu S (2019) The influence of artificial intelligence development on patent legislation. In: Proceedings of the 2019 international conference on robots and intelligent system (ICRIS). IEEE, pp 110–113. https://doi.org/10.1109/ICRIS.2019.00036
170. Gunes Peschke S, Peschke L (2022) Artificial intelligence and the new challenges for EU legislation. YBHD 11, 1267. https://doi.org/10.33432/ybuhukuk.1104344
171. Horowitz MC, Allen GC, Kania EB, Scharre P (2018) Strategic competition in an era of artificial intelligence. Center for a New American Security
172. Mirzazadeh I (2022) Artificial intelligence (AI) and violation of human rights. Available at SSRN 4310188. https://doi.org/10.2139/ssrn.4310188
173. Chae Y (2020) US AI regulation guide: legislative overview and practical considerations. J Robot Artif Intell Law 3:2753. https://doi.org/10.3316/agispt.20230202082753
174. Neves M (2022) From symbolic legislation, a forward-moving debate. In: Kevin M (ed) Symbolic constitutionalization (Oxford). https://doi.org/10.1093/oso/9780192857149.003.0002
175. Přibáň J (2016) On legal symbolism in symbolic legislation: a systems theoretical perspective. In: Symbolic legislation theory and developments in Biolaw, pp 105–121. https://doi.org/10.1007/978-3-319-33365-6_7
176. van Klink B (2014) Symbolic legislation: an essentially political concept. In: van Klink B, van Beers B, Poort L (eds) Symbolic legislation theory and new developments in Biolaw, Springer 2015 Forthcoming, VU University Amsterdam Legal Studies Paper Series. https://doi.org/10.2139/ssrn.2540471
177. Königs P (2022) Artificial intelligence and responsibility gaps: what is the problem? Ethics Inform Technol 24(3):36. https://doi.org/10.1007/s10676-022-09643-0
178. Hall MI (2005) Duty, causation, and third-party perpetrators: the bonnie Mooney case. McGill LJ 50:597
179. Melia MC (2007) Victims and self-liability in criminal law: beyond contributive negligence and foreseeability (without blaming the victim). Pace L Rev 28:739
180. Kowert W (2017) The foreseeability of human-artificial intelligence interactions. Tex Law Rev 96:181
181. Claussén Karlsson M (2017) Artificial intelligence and the external element of the crime: an analysis of the liability problem (dissertation). https://urn.kb.se/resolve?urn=urn:nbn:se:oru:diva-58269
182. Lehmann J, Breuker J, Brouwer B (2004) Causation in AI and law. Artif Intell Law 12:279–315. https://doi.org/10.1007/s10506-005-4157-y
183. Fletcher GP (2017) The theory of criminal negligence: a comparative analysis. In: The structure and limits of criminal law. Routledge, pp 441–478
184. Herstein OJ (2010) Responsibility in negligence: why the duty of care is not a duty "to try." Can J Law Jurisp 23(2):403–428. https://doi.org/10.1017/S0841820900004987
185. Storey T (2018) Gross negligence manslaughter, restaurant owners and the duty of care: R v Zaman [2017] EWCA Crim 1783. J Crim Law 82(3):201–205. https://doi.org/10.1177/0022018318779488
186. Carter D (2020) Regulation and ethics in artificial intelligence and machine learning technologies: Where are we now? Who is responsible? Can the information professional play a role? Bus Inform Rev 37(2):60–68. https://doi.org/10.1177/0266382120923962
187. Li J, Liu Y, Yue L, Jin F, Guo Q, Xu C (2018) Artificial intelligence governed by laws and regulations. In: Reconstructing our orders: artificial intelligence and human society, pp 61–97. https://doi.org/10.1007/978-981-13-2209-9_3

188. O'Sullivan S, Nevejans N, Allen C, Blyth A, Leonard S, Pagallo U et al (2019) Legal, regulatory, and ethical frameworks for development of standards in artificial intelligence (AI) and autonomous robotic surgery. Int J Med Robot Comput Assist Surg 15(1):e1968. https://doi.org/10.1002/rcs.1968
189. Ramraj VV (1999) A theory of criminal negligence. University of Toronto, Toronto
190. Sibai FN (2020) AI crimes: a classification. In: Proceedings of the 2020 international conference on cyber security and protection of digital services (cyber security). IEEE, pp 1–8. https://doi.org/10.1109/CyberSecurity49315.2020.9138891

Chapter 3
Imputation System for Negligence Crime Involving AI

The theoretical premise of responding to the imputation gaps for negligence crimes involving AI has in fact set the theoretical direction for bridging the imputation gaps. That is to say, on the premise of not overturning the traditional system of criminal law theory, the theoretical dilemma of this imputation is realized through the re-understanding of the imputation system. Influenced by the theory of ontological imputation, some opinions advocate that the gaps in imputation should be dealt with by lowering the standard of the perpetrator's duty of foresight and avoidance [1, 2]. However, this has fundamentally overcome the theoretical dilemma brought about by AI technology to the imputation for the negligence crime, but is only a helpless compromise to the present situation of the inability to foresee in the negligence crime involving AI. Therefore, only by shifting the imputation for the negligence crimes from an ontological to a normative theory is it possible to address such gaps in the imputation for negligence crimes involving AI.

3.1 Imputation for Negligence Crime

According to the conclusions of the previous arguments in this study, the challenges that AI technology poses to criminal law norms are mainly focused on the imputation gap for negligence crime involving AI. According to the traditional criminal law theory, the basis of liability for negligent crime is the will factor such as the perpetrator's foreseeability, but the "participation" of AI technology in the crime has already shaken such imputation basis for negligent crime [3, 4]. Therefore, the reasonable direction of theoretical efforts should be to transform the system of imputation for the negligence crime in order to avoid the reliance of negligence on the element of subjective will, thereby achieving a theoretical transformation from will imputation to norm imputation.

S. Zhao, *Principle of Criminal Imputation for Negligence Crime Involving Artificial Intelligence*, Artificial Intelligence and the Rule of Law,
https://doi.org/10.1007/978-981-97-0722-5_3

3.1.1 Ontological Structure of Unlawfulness

In philosophy, ontology is the theory used to discuss the roots of the universe, and the existence of God. However, it was not until German criminal law scholar Welzel introduced ontology into criminal law methodology in the twentieth century that ontology began to influence the development of criminal law science [5–7]. According to his understanding, values and norms can be derived from facts and existence. In contrast with ontology theory, normative theory in criminal law is a framework that seeks to establish ethical and moral principles as the basis for formulating, interpreting, and applying laws in the realm of criminal justice. Neo-Kantian philosophy holds that norms can only be derived from value system rather than from objective reality [8, 9]. The fundamental dispute between ontology and normative theory lies in which level the persons are placed in the relationship between norms, individuals, and society [10, 11]. In fact, only in a normative society can individual people become social beings with rights and obligations. In this kind of society, the social beings are persons, which evolve from the individual. To a certain extent, human beings are both natural persons and social persons.

It is precisely because of the ontological and axiological understanding of person that the imputation can be divided into subjective imputation and objective imputation. In the subjective imputation, will of the person is the starting point of such imputation. According to this, the imputation does not lie in the state of infringement of legal interests, but because that state is a manifestation of human free will [12, 13]. In fact, the subject and its personal will in the ontological sense are important contents of imputation. Therefore, the structural system of unlawfulness in the negligence crimes cannot be separated from ontology. Moreover, it is also given an axiological aspect.

As the link between the act and the perpetrator, the will is the key factor in determining the unlawfulness and culpability of the act [14, 15]. The reason why the unlawfulness can be attributed to the actor is that the act reflects the free will of the actor and can be evaluated by the norm and moral. Influenced by the imputation theory from Pufendorf, Kant also advocated freedom of will as the basis for imputation, and regarded it as the basis of human behavior [16, 17]. In this regard, Hegel believed that will was the element that could explain why the unlawfulness was attributed to the subject. This is because the will connects the body and the mind and is also the expression and basis of the existence of "I" [18, 19]. As a subjective attitude toward possible outcomes, the will of the person creates meaningful control over its behavior. In this regard, the causal flow of the behavior is manipulated by the will of the actor.

In the intentional crimes, the will of the perpetrator is manifested as a "hope for" or "indifference to" the occurrence of those consequences. This kind of will is contrary to the norms. Therefore, the normative condemnation of perpetrator in the intentional crime stems from the subjective abuse of his own freedom of will. Unlike "hope for" or "indifference to" occurrence of the consequences in the case of intentional crimes, the will of the perpetrator in negligent crimes is to "oppose" the occurrence of harmful results. Therefore, if the will element alone is taken into account, the perpetrator does not have subjective malignancy, but rather should be promoted by the norms of the law. However, if we look at the cognitive element, the cognitive possibility in the negligent crime is the evaluation of the scope of what the actor can recognize, which is obviously beyond the scope of the evaluation of the actor's own ability. Therefore, in the strict sense, it is not a kind of awareness of the perpetrator, and it does not belong to the category of cognitive elements. For this reason, it is generally recognized in theory that negligence crime cannot be explained at all from an ontological perspective.

As a result, the actors in such crime can only apply normative attribution of his responsibility, that is, to fill the lack of subjective aspects of the negligent offenders from the perspective of normative theory [20, 21]. For example, according to the theory of objective attribution, an objective act is the unlawfulness in the negligence crime if it deviates from what is expected by the norm of law and creates and realizes a risk not permitted by the law. As a result, this theory fundamentally abandons the consideration of the subjective illegal element of the offender in the judgment of negligent wrongfulness [22, 23].

However, it is difficult to provide a legitimate basis for the criminal attribution to the actor without the will of the actor, because a person should never act merely as a means to achieve the goals of others. If the will of the actor is not taken into account and the normative expectations of the citizen are emphasized, then the citizen may be reduced to a tool of the State's domination. So, how should we correctly evaluate the will element in the attribution of liability in case of negligent crimes? In this regard, it has been argued that the free will in the context of negligence crime is manifested in the actor's abandonment of self-determination with respect to the conduct that relates to the occurrence of the result [24–26]. In case of negligence crime, if the perpetrator had been able to make use of his ability to foresee and avoid the occurrence of the consequence, he could have avoided it.

As a result, the basis of the actor's liability lies in the fact that he did not make full use of his ability to foresee the result, thereby putting himself in a state in which he was unable to make his own decisions. In fact, giving up self-determination is a subjective psychology in the ontological sense of negligent crimes, and this is closely related to the actor's ability to pay attention, so it belongs to the ontological content of the actor [27, 28].

3.1.2 Axiological Structure of Unlawfulness

In the intentional crimes, self-determination is the decision of a person who recognizes the danger and explicitly endangers the legal interest. In contrast, self-determination in the negligence crime is a decision by the perpetrator to forget the legal interest because he does not recognize the danger. However, if such a psychological attitude in the ontological sense has not been axiologically evaluated, its content will have no meaning for the unlawfulness of the negligence crime.

From the perspective of teleological behavior theory, the purpose is the connection between the actor and its harmful results. However, this purpose actually only has an ontological significance, so normative evaluation is not the focus of this teleological behavior theory [29, 30]. However, in the view of the normative theorists such as Jakobs, since the free will is difficult to define the liability, it cannot bear the burden to demonstrate the necessity and legitimacy of penalty, [31]. For Jakobs, an actor is liable only if he is obligated to the validity of a legal norm. However, this argument is based only on the criminal law function, so that such purely normative judgment without the ontological sense is not reasonable for understanding the unlawfulness. In the crime of negligence, the ontological wrongfulness is manifested in the actor allowing himself to fall into a state in which he cannot make his own decisions.

However, if we want to further clarify this state, judgment and discussion in the normative theory sense are indispensable [32, 33]. In the old negligence theory, the normative nature of unlawfulness is not obvious, because the judgment of the duty of care in such theory is centered on the obligation to foresee the consequences. Normally, in this kind of unlawfulness judgment, the possibility to foresee something is a judgment based on empirical facts, and the social equivalence is an important content of its judgment [26, 34, 35]. In this judgment, the equivalence means that the occurrence of the result caused by the behavior is general and normal in daily life. Therefore, the decisive content of the equivalence in the theory of causality is the foreseeable possibility.

Compared with the old negligence theory, the new theory emphasizes the obligation of the actor to avoid the consequences, and its purpose is to limit the scope of the obligation to foresee the occurrence of consequences. In fact, the violation of the obligation to avoid the consequences means that the actor fails to act prudently in accordance with the requirements of the norms of care, thereby deviating from the requirements of the norms [2, 36]. In the negligence crime, the perpetrator violates a requirement of care imposed by the legal order on every prudent and reasonable members of society for which the perpetrator has its foreseeability. Therefore, the key to the actor's violation of the obligation to avoid the consequences is that the harmful results are caused by the violation of this obligation. This judgment must be inseparable from the protective purpose of the norm [37, 38]. If the actor violated his duty of care and caused a harmful result, but this result would have occurred even if he had complied with the duty of care, the attribution to the actor should be excluded at the normative level. The main reason for this is the protective purpose of the norm [39].

In this respect, the actor in the negligence crime is judged not on the basis of what he actually did, but on the extent to which he deviated from the standard of ordinary human conduct. Thus, the attribution of will in the ontological sense and attribution of norms at the normative level assume the different functions. The former attributes the result to the actor, while the latter attributes the result to the act. A specific result can be evaluated in the legal sense only if that result is objectively realized in a manner consistent with the normative purpose. In other words, the risk of act is of criminal law significance only if such act is relevant to the result of the constituent elements.

3.2 Shift in Imputation from Will to Norm

After explaining the unlawfulness of the negligence crimes from the ontological and normative perspectives, it is necessary to discuss in detail the imputation structure of negligence crime, with the purpose to provide a more reasonable theory to deal with the gaps in the of imputation for the negligence crimes involving AI.

3.2.1 Will and Will Imputation

The basis for the will imputation is the free will possessed by the human being. In such imputation, the object of criminal condemnation is the will of the offender, while his objective behavior evaluated against the norms of the law still belongs to the external manifestation of his will in its essence. In this regard, some have argued that the responsibility of the offender is based not on the legally prohibited state of affairs that he objectively created, but rather on the fact that such state is a manifestation of his free will, i.e., that it was caused by the actor of the offender, who has owned the free will [40–42].

In the theoretical development, the theory of will imputation has always been associated with the names of Hegel, Larenz, and Honig [13, 43, 44]. The premise for Hegel to attribute responsibility to the free will is that he believes that people have the free will [45, 46]. Therefore, only people who have owned free will can become subjects in the criminal law, and the actus reus can only be attributed because its actor is the fault of his will. According to idea from Hegel, a person can be a subject of the crime because he has free will, and his act is only an objective manifestation of his free will. In short, it is the free will that determines the possibility of the existence of the subject and the attribution of the conduct to this subject.

On the basis of imputation theory from Hegel, Larenz identified that the central problem of imputation is to address what the actor should be held responsible for, i.e., what can be counted as the actor's own behavior [47]. In this regard, Larenz distinguishes between causation and objective imputation. According to his idea, the causation theory addresses the problem of the empirical link between the act and its result, whereas imputation theory discusses how to determine that an act can be attributed to a particular subject. Thus, causation alone cannot solve the problem of the imputation of conduct [43, 45]. On this premise, Larenz attributes the act to the subject by introducing the concept of act purpose. Because of the teleological consistency of the actor, Larenz believes that it can be used to determine whether the behavior belongs to the actor himself. Accordingly, whether or not the actor has the possibility to foresee his own act is the prerequisite and basis for the attribution of conduct to the subject. In the imputation theory of Larenz, the foreseeability has become a fundamental principle for the imputation.

Similar to Larenz, another scholar, Honig, also argues that the two elements of causation and objective attribution belong to the different theoretical levels of the relationship between act and its results [5, 48]. Accordingly, causation describes an ontologically objective link between the act and its result, and is therefore a factual element. The objective attribution, however, gives the legal significance to the objective link between act and its result at the legal level, thus making it an element of responsibility that can carry legal evaluation [49, 50]. With regard to the relationship between the act and its result, Honig distinguishes between causation and objective attribution, and also considers the causation to be the prerequisite for the objective attribution. However, how can the act be attributed to its subject in the sense of legal evaluation? In this regard, Honig proposes the concept of objective purposiveness [5, 42]. According to such understanding, only the results that can be considered purposive are objectively attributable. From this it can be seen that Honig is also looking for an objective link between the subject, the act and the result, and this link is the basis of the value judgment. Therefore, the imputation of act and its results is not only the factual evaluation, but also a normative evaluation.

On the basis of Hegel's thought, the will imputation theory, through the continuous development of Larenz, Honig and others has formed the imputation theory with rich content. Although the direction of such theoretical development is different, this imputation theory, on the whole, has the following main aspects: firstly, this ontological imputation is based on free will of the actor. Whether it is Hegel, Larenz, or Honig, they all believe that only a person who possesses his free will can be an offender in the criminal law, and therefore only his behavior under the dominion of his free will can be the condemnation object from the criminal law [41, 51–53]. In other words, the essence of negative evaluation from the criminal law is the condemnation of the free will of the actor. In this sense, whether a person should take criminal responsibility depends on his free will, rather than on the objective factors such as externalized behavior.

Secondly, the basis for this will imputation is the foreseeable possibility of the actor. Within the scope of the knowledge and intention of the actor, his foreseeable possibility is the connection point between the act and his behavior that can be attributed [54, 55]. Only when the actor has the foreseeable possibility of his act and the results can he use his will to control this act and promote the occurrence of its results. Therefore, in this imputation of will, the foreseeable possibility of the actor is the basis or premise of the imputation. In this regard, although some argue that the foreseeable possibility of the actor, understood objectively, is biased in favor of the act and the result and away from the free will of the perpetrator, what is embodied in the realized result is what is directed by his will [56, 57]. Objectively, it is only on this basis that it can be justified why the perpetrator is responsible for this result that occurs in the external world. Thirdly, it is on the basis of the will imputation that the theory of objective imputation has been developed. In terms of the theoretical development of the objective imputation, the corresponding theory from Larenz and Honig are based on the theory of will imputation from Hegel. The theory of imputation as formulated by Larenz itself reflects the move towards the objectification of the elements of imputation, while the objective purposefulness proposed by Honig is also considered to be the fundamental determinant of the imputation [12, 13].

Although these theories still rely on the subjective elements and will elements in the nature of responsibility attribution, Larenz and Honig attempted to realize the transformation from subjectivity to objectivity by abstracting individuals into ordinary people regarding the possibility of foresight [58, 59]. Thus, the imputation of will does not imply a purely subjective imputation. In such imputation, the objective element of the imputation in fact still plays a role. However, free will remains the most important element for the attribution of the criminal responsibility. Within the scope of will imputation, the will as the basis and object of condemnation can inevitably lead to the tendency of the overall imputation structure to be dominated by the subjective elements.

How should we evaluate the theory of will imputation?

Firstly, the theoretical development and principal content of will imputation show that the will imputation realizes the distinction between facts and norms in the field of criminal law. For people, their behavior is both a natural and a social activity. From a factual perspective, causality can only show that there is a causal relationship between human behavior and results in the sense of natural laws, but it cannot attribute the results of behavior to the actor at the normative level. Simply put, causality cannot achieve the attribution of responsibility for the results. As a result, some viewpoints hold that only the act and its result that are governed by the free will of the person will can be attributed to the actor. According to their understanding, the basis for attribution is not causation at the factual level, but the collusion between the actor, his behavior, and the result, as realized by the will.

Thus, the proponents of the will imputation theory argue for the exclusion of ontological causation from the imputation [60, 61]. On this premise, some views further advocate the concretization of free will as the possibility to foresee something [62, 63]. That is to say, only the acts and its results that the actor can foresee have the possibility of being governed by his free will. In order to establish some non-normative evaluative and general standards for the imputation, some views have abstracted the possibility of foreseeing or manipulating possibilities into the objective standards for the imputation [56, 64]. From these theoretical endeavors, it is clear that the will imputation itself is not the result of normative evaluation, nor is it the content of normative evaluation. Thus, the will imputation merely provides a precondition for the normative evaluation. In the case of attribution of responsibility, the will imputation provides a general theoretical basis for the imputation in the criminal law.

Secondly, this will imputation, which lacks the decisive normative evaluation, undoubtedly results in an overreliance on the subjective element in the criminal imputation. For example, in negligence crimes, the traditional view is that the basis for the imputation is whether the perpetrator has his foreseeability [65, 66]. This is to concretize the abstract theory of the foreseeability, which is used in the will imputation to illustrate the scope of free will and the connection between the actor and his behavior, into a concrete criterion for determining whether or not to attribute the responsibility. This causes the possibility of foreseeability, which was originally a prerequisite element of normative evaluation, to participate in normative evaluation, thus making the traditional negligence theory rely heavily on subjective elements.

In particular, when dealing with the gaps in the imputation for the negligence crimes involving AI, since the subjective elements such as foreseeability of the perpetrator are subject to great uncertainty with the influence of technological risks, the imputation, which relies excessively on the subjective elements of will imputation inevitably affect the reasonable judgment of criminal liability. As a result, part of the criminal liability for the negligence crimes involving AI cannot objectively be effectively and reasonably attributed to the appropriate subject of the crime.

3.2.2 *Norm and Normative Imputation*

In contrast to the will imputation, normative imputation is the idea of imputation based on the legal norms. The basis for the attribution of unlawfulness to the offender lies in the violation of the norm by the perpetrator. In the will imputation, the free will of the offender is central to the consideration of imputation, whereas in normative imputation, the core of it is the violation of the norm against which the unlawfulness was committed. Since this kind of imputation is closely related to norm violations, this theory is called normative imputation. In the normative attribution, the risk that the act brings to the legal order has become the key concept connecting facts and norms, because the risk itself is a normative evaluation of the factual state. To some extent, various doctrines in the normative imputation revolve around the recognition and definition of risk.

Theoretically, there stands a close relationship between the normative imputation and adequacy. The theoretical premise of the theory of adequacy is: the causal relationship between things is one of the reflection forms of the universal connection and mutual restriction of things, so it is objective and independent of people's consciousness, and it does not depend on the will of people [67, 68]. Subject to the level of human knowledge, the complexity of the connection between things, the limited nature of human cognitive ability, etc., it is impossible for people to fully understand the causal relationship between things. Thus, the determination of causality is not entirely a process of logical deduction, but only a process of possibility judgment. According to this understanding, the judgment of causality first needs to determine whether the conditions for the occurrence of the result are indispensable for the occurrence of the damage, and then determine whether there is an adequacy causation between the act and the result [69–71].

Starting from the theory of adequacy, some views argue that causation addresses the link between behavior and its result at the factual level, while the theory of adequacy evaluates such relationship at the normative level. Therefore, some arguments tried to use the violation of norms as the basis for imputation, and such understanding laid the foundation for normative imputation [72, 73]. In line with the previous discussion, the theory of adequacy generally assumes that the causation between an act and its result is equivalent only if the act is capable of causing the result to occur or enhancing the likelihood of the result occurring in a general sense.

Indeed, whether an act is equivalent to an outcome is itself a further value judgment at the normative level.

In determining whether there is adequacy, some views oppose the use of life experience as the standard for determining whether the outcome is equivalent for the act. Instead, they argue in favor of using norms as the standard, and that the damages of norms must be taken into account when judging the risk of the outcome occurring as elevated [74, 75]. In this judgment, the corresponding norm establishes both behavioral prohibitions that are used to prevent some elevated risk, and at the same time identifies the important legally significant boundaries that are used to delineate the purpose of the norm. In that case, if the behavior has violated the normative prohibition of the risk-escalation, the actor may be held liable. However, if the behavior has not violated the purpose established in the norm and the it is beneficial to the society, the actor should not be held liable because the risk in question is a permissible risk [76, 77].

In the adequacy judgment, some views advocate that two kinds of adequacy judgments are used to determine whether there is an attributable connection between the norm violation and the occurrence of the result. Among them, the key to the first judgment is whether the actor must behave objectively and prudently. In this case, the behavior of the actor is norm-violating only if the he lacks the objectively necessary caution to avoid the outcome that must be avoided by him [78, 79].

Generally speaking, the so-called violation of "objectively necessary caution" means that the behavior significantly increases the risk of achieving the result. In this dual equivalence judgment, the key to the link between norm violation and outcome is the realization of the prohibited risks, which is also the focus of normative imputation. Indeed, whereas the first relevance determination was to account for the attribution of responsibility between the normative violation and the abstract result by means of "objectively necessary caution", while the second was to account for the link of responsibility between the normative violation and the concrete result by means of "prohibiting the realization of the risk". It can be seen that the fundamental purpose of this view is to try to determine the normative correlation between the norm violation of the behavior and the outcome through two judgments of adequacy.

In the theoretical development of normative imputation, the view represented by Jakobs takes the preservation of the validity of legal norms as the basis of his idea of imputation [12, 48]. According to this view, people are related to each other as the role-bearers in their everyday life and can rely on others to perform a normatively expected behavior. What the society restricts is not the individual, but the person. Only in the society can the individual become person and play his corresponding roles in the society. In fact, society expects different normative behaviors from each person according to the different social roles he plays, and these behavioral expectations form the norms [80, 81]. Criminal law punishes those who violate norms, not because their behavior infringes upon the legal interests, but because they violate normative expectations of behavior, and therefore society needs to impose penalties for this in order to stabilize the general expectations of behavior of the public.

Fundamentally, the basis of criminal imputation lies in the breach of the legal order and norms by the offender. Thus, the basic task of criminal law is to preserve the validity of norms as a stabilizing social order, and the penalty is the price to be borne by the violator of the norm for his negation of the norm, that is, the negation of the norm validity [12, 82]. For person in society, in order to ensure the effective realization of their social interaction, the person has a certain obligation to guarantee his own behavior. What the law regulates is this kind of behavior that violates guarantee obligations and thus fails the reasonable expectations of others. On this basis, Jakobs takes the forbidden risks as the prerequisite for the imputation, and takes the "social role" as the criterion for judging such forbidden risks.

Unlike Jakobs, who understands criminal unlawfulness as violation of normative validity, his student Pawlik understands it as a violation of the obligation of citizens to cooperate in the defense of their freedom in the society [83]. Thus, the violation by citizen of his obligation to cooperate in the defense of freedom is the basis for imputation. A free state can persist only because its citizens are, by and large, free to obey the law, and the violations of the law are isolated phenomena. This is at the heart of the cooperated obligation of citizens to the existing state of law. Indeed, the law represents an expectation of behavior in the society, and citizens who act in accordance with the law embody the validity of the law [84]. It is the validity of norms that helps the individual citizens overcome the fundamental risk of violating them [85, 86]. Therefore, in order to accomplish this task, the citizens rely on the reciprocal behavior of another person. In this way, the law-abiding citizens perform their role as citizens in opposite ways to the law-breakers: the latter declares the invalidity of the norms by their own decisions and actions, while the former recognizes the universal validity of the norms [83, 87].

It follows that criminal law, as Pawlik understands it, is nothing other than the norms that require citizens to fulfill this duty of concerted effort to preserve the freedom in the society. The quality of criminal unlawfulness lies in the fact that the perpetrator violates his duty of cooperation in maintaining the existing legal status, thereby undermining his role as a representative of the legal community—in short, his role as a citizen [83]. In short, citizens' violation of their own obligation to cooperate in the defense of freedom is the basis for their imputation.

On the basis of imputation theory from Karl Engisch, Roxin has further developed a theory of elevated risk in his normative imputation [88, 89]. In this normative imputation, the theory of elevated risk rests on the distinction between the permitted and prohibited risks. According to Roxin, the permitted risk is the result of a trade-off between the need for interaction and the interests of individual protection [56, 90]. Today, in our modern society, some risks will always accompany the development of society. However, for some risks that are beneficial to social development, such as the modern transportation, dangerous instruments and equipment, etc., the perpetrator can only be held responsible when the risks created by his actions exceed the permitted limit. According to the trade-off criterion, the risk exceeding the permissible limits of the legislation naturally falls into the category of prohibited risk, whereas the permitted risks are those caused by actions within the legal limit. With this promise, Roxin further discusses the significance of reducing the risk versus creating a new, lower risk in the context of objective attribution exclusion. With regard to the realization of risk, Roxin argues that the prohibited risk is realized in the result if the breach of the obligation makes the risk of the result higher than its permission. From this it can be seen that risk elevation actually consists of both the risk creation and realization, and this constitutes the backbone of the objective imputation theory from Roxin [91].

In the risk elevation theory, it has been argued that the theory of the protective purpose of norms should be introduced into judgments about the realization of risk [92, 93]. According to this view, the result should not be regarded as a mere objective fact in terms of the criminal constituent elements, but rather the result should be regarded as whether or not it is one of those results that can be understood by the norms of prudence. Therefore, there is a realization of a risk if the protective purpose of the breached norm of prudence covers a specific occurrence of the result [94, 95]. In this sense, the significance of the protective purpose of norms is not merely to account for the increased risk, but is a normative criterion for judging the realization of risk. The protective purpose of the norm thus becomes an important element in the theory of objective imputation.

Although theories differ in their understanding of the normative imputation, they all weaken the over-reliance of imputation on the subjective factor of the will from the perpetrator, thus attempting to construct a logical system and method of criminal imputation at the more explicit level of normative violation. Specifically, the following are the basic requirements for this normative imputation.

Firstly, different types of risk should be rationally distinguished and identified. In the normative imputation, the term "risk" has become the core vocabulary of the theoretical construction and argumentation of imputation [73, 96]. Risk itself describes the normative relationship between behavior and results, which has already reflected the importance of norms in the criminal imputation. In fact, the normative imputation is based on the term "risk" as the logical starting point to develop the theory of criminal imputation [97, 98]. In modern society, risks are inevitable and even difficult to prevent. In order to maintain the effective function of the society itself, as well as its progress and development, certain risks with the capacity to achieve these social utilities should be permitted by law, and such risks are the permitted risks [96, 99].

However, when the occurrence of a certain risk breaks the balance between the social utility and social harm, and thus exceeds the level of public tolerance and social expectations, then the law should regulate such risk. This kind of risk is named the prohibited risk in the criminal imputation. From the perspective of the normative imputation theory, the permitted risks are not the object of the normative evaluation, because it is the price to be paid for the society if it can maintain its orderly operation and development. Only those behavior that has realized a prohibited risk may be imputed. Therefore, how to reasonably distinguish between permitted and prohibited risks in accordance with criminal law is a prerequisite for the normative imputation [100, 101].

Secondly, how to decide the prohibited risk plays the leading role in the normative imputation. After distinguishing between the permitted risks and prohibited risks according to criminal law, the normative attribution requires further judgment on the existence of prohibited risks. The behavior is of normative evaluative significance only if it has the normatively prohibited risk [102, 103]. In other words, the existence of prohibited risk actually gives behavior that exists at the factual level the possibility of evaluation at the normative level. However, how can the existence of a prohibited risk in the behavior be determined? In this regard, the normative imputation theory regards the breach of the duty of care as central to this kind of determination [104, 105].

For the duty of care, it belongs to the normative standard in the imputation, and it is the criminal law norms that are its main normative source. In the case of the prohibited risks, the concept of the risk corresponds to the standards established by the norms of behavior that describe the legal interests protected against illegal infringement by the criminal law norms. Indeed, a violation of duty of care by the perpetrator implies that there is a prohibited risk of his behavior. Therefore, in the normative imputation, the actor may be imputed only if he has violated his duty of care and his behavior posed a prohibited risk [106, 107].

Thirdly, the normative imputation presupposes that the prohibited risk is realized within the scope of norm's protective purpose. The realization of prohibited risk is the fundamental requirement for normative imputation for the results caused by the behavior, which also illustrates the normative connection between the behavior and its result with the normative imputation. That is to say, the prohibited risk of the behavior needs to be ultimately realized in the purpose of the normative protection, so that the behavior and its result have a normative connection [108, 109]. Therefore, how to judge the realization of results is at the core of the objective imputation. What needs to be determined is whether the risk that is realized in the outcome is a prohibited risk. In this regard, some theories argue that only risks that have normative significance for the realization of the results are risks prohibited by law. Another part of the view is that only the risks whose results are realized within the protective purpose of the norm are those risks prohibited by law. Although these two kinds of views are different, they both indicate the importance of risk realization in the normative imputation theory. To some extent, the relationship between behavior and its result, risk and harm, in a normative sense, focuses on the process of risk realization, so that the realization of normative imputation necessarily requires a rational judgment of the realization of prohibited risks.

Normative imputation is based on the criminal norm, which is the most fundamental difference between the normative imputation and the will imputation. In this kind of imputation, taking norms as the basis mainly provides the following three criteria for the normative imputation: First, norms are used as the criterion for classifying permitted or prohibited risks; second, norms are used as the criterion for judging whether the behavior contains the attribute of the prohibited risks; third, norms are used as the criterion for judging the realization of the prohibited risks [108, 110]. With the help of these three criteria, the norms play the structural role in the criminal imputation, which not only reduces the excessive reliance on subjective elements such as the will in the imputation, but also expands the scope of evaluation of criminal law norms. It is on this basis that the elements of imputation, such as act, result and causation, have been transformed from the system of description at the factual level into the system of evaluation at the normative level.

For objective imputation, the core issue to be solved is, under what preconditions, the results that have occurred can be regarded as the work of the perpetrator and be attributed to him. Regarding this issue, the theory of will imputation identifies an objective criterion of purposiveness with pre-legal significance, while the normative imputation emphasizes the decisive significance of the existing norms in the judgments of the criminal imputation [111, 112]. Although the objects of evaluation in the normative imputation still comes from the acts and results at the factual level, the corresponding normative evaluation requires that there be a normative connection between the objects of evaluation. This requires the evaluation of factual act, result, and its causation in a normative sense, so as to exclude the accidental situations that do not have legal evaluation significance [97, 113]. In this sense, through the normative evaluation, normative imputation ultimately achieves the judgment of the entire process of prohibited risk from its creation to its occurrence of result at the normative level. Its fundamental purpose is to exclude from the imputation those things that do not have normative evaluation significance.

3.3 Structure of Imputation for Negligence Crime

According to the conclusion of the previous argument in this study, the challenge of development and application of AI to the traditional imputation theory is mainly in the gaps in the imputation for the negligence crime involving AI. It is because of this gap that the criminal liability for the negligence crimes involving AI cannot be effectively assigned according to the traditional theory. Therefore, how to adjust the imputation structure to meet the practical needs of liability for negligence crimes involving AI is the core issue that this study will focus on solving in the following part. The first issue to be addressed here is the fundamental question of whether the traditional imputation structure of the negligence crime is based on will or normative imputation.

3.3.1 Ideal Imputation Structure

With regard to the essential attribute of the criminal imputation, according to the previous discussion, the will imputation is to make the human will the core of imputation. The key to determining whether to be liable is not the legally prohibited state caused by the act, but whether the act itself can be regarded as the work of the perpetrator's will [13, 114, 115]. The theory of the will imputation presupposes that human behavior is determined by his motivation, which is conceived as a process of psychological mechanisms [110, 116]. Accordingly, the external causal process is only the external manifestation of this psychological process, which constitutes the object of volitional domination. Thus, the will of the subject not only constitutes the connection between the act and the perpetrator, but also becomes the determining factor in the unlawfulness of the act.

Within the framework of will imputation, the subjective perception of the perpetrator is decisive for the attribution. This is because an act can only be considered malicious and ethically reprehensible if the perpetrator is determined to commit his behavior despite the fact that he is aware that it will lead to harmful consequences prohibited by the criminal law [53, 117]. Unlike the basis of will imputation, normative imputation centers on the violation of a norm. The goal of this imputation is to achieve a limitation of the liability of the perpetrator in the direction of the normative protective purpose that has been damaged. Accordingly, the key to the determination of imputation lies not in the subjective will of the perpetrator at the time of the commission of his offence, but in the risk objectively posed to others or to society by the violation of the norm [112]. Thus, the objective threat or infringement of the legal interest caused by the act is the decisive factor in determining the attribution of responsibility to the perpetrator.

According to the general theoretical understanding, a negligent crime refers to an act committed by a person who should have foreseen that his act would possibly entail harmful consequences to society but who fails to do so through his negligence or, having foreseen the consequences, readily believes that they can be avoided, so that the consequences do occur [2, 118]. As far as the normative structure of the negligence crime is concerned, the traditional negligence crime is structured in the context of the subjective aspect of the crime, which does not involve the objective aspect of it. In this theoretical framework, the possibility of foreseeing becomes the premise and foundation of the duty of foreseeing and avoidance, which is also the embodiment of the responsibility doctrine in the traditional negligence crime [119, 120]. According to the basic content of such doctrine, the acts of the perpetrator can only be imputed to the perpetrator on the premise of capacity for responsibility and intent or negligence. That is to say, the attribution of responsibility to the perpetrator presupposes not only that the perpetrator has the capacity for criminal responsibility, but also that his behavior must have been committed with intent or negligence [26, 56].

For the negligence crime, why does the perpetrator need to be negligent for his behavior if he should take the criminal liability?

In the case of negligence, since the perpetrator himself does not have the active will to promote the occurrence of the harmful results, his domination over the offence and its causal process can only be manifested in the awareness of these factors, i.e., his ability to foresee them beforehand. Only when the perpetrator is able to foresee the possible results of his behavior and the direction of the factual causal process, he has the possibility to control the development of events. In the case of negligence crime, the possibility of foreseeability implies the possibility of domination, and kind of possibility implies correspondingly the possibility of the responsibility [121, 122]. Thus, it is the possibility of foreseeability that forms the core of the theoretical framework of the traditional negligence crime. Whether it is "should have foreseen" or "have foreseen", the premise is that the actor can foresee, that is, the actor has the possibility of foreseeability [66, 123]. In fact, the creation and violation of the duty of care has always been used in theory as the analytical framework for the negligence crime. According to this understanding, the crime of negligence is a violation by the perpetrator of his duty of care, which includes the duty to foresee the result and to avoid the result. The failure of the perpetrator to fulfill his duty to avoid the result is the objective constituent element of the negligence crime, while the violation of his duty of care means that he has the foreseeable possibility of the result [124, 125].

It can be seen that for negligence crimes, the perpetrator's foreseeability of the harmful results is the minimum requirement for the combination of his will and behavior. In addition, the possibility of his foresight is the foundation of the theory and the primary condition for judging the establishment of the crime. Therefore, only when the perpetrator has the possibility of foresight, the attribution of responsibility can be justified. This imputation structure, which takes the possibility of foresight as the center of the negligence crime, still focuses on the subjective psychological level in its understanding of this kind of crime. Therefore, it is a structure of will imputation in nature.

However, it is precisely because of this will imputation structure of the negligence crime that it creates the gaps in response to the imputation for the negligence crime involving AI. The question is, in order to deal with such imputation gap, what should be the imputation structure of the negligence crime? This can be further illustrated by analogy with the imputation structure of intentional crimes. In such crime, the perpetrator has the obvious will that is hostile to the norms of law, and this kind of will determines the unlawfulness of his act. Therefore, the will of the perpetrator becomes the object of normative condemnation, and the imputation structure based on the will is in fact the judgment of the will of the perpetrator [52, 126, 127].

In contrast, the perpetrator of negligence crime does not subjectively wish to be an enemy of the law; he does not desire or even reject the outcome of the crime. Therefore, subjectively, there stands no will factor worthy of negative evaluation by legal norms in the negligence crime. The real reason for the condemnation in the negligence crime lies in the perpetrator's violation of his duty of care created by the norm of law, and the resulting damage to the legal interest is realized within the protective purpose of the norm of law. In short, it is not the will of the perpetrator that counts in the case of negligence crime, but rather the fact that the act itself deviates from the standard of the rational person expected by the legal norm and thus objectively poses the prohibited risk to the legal interest [96, 108].

This leads to the conclusion that the basis of imputation for negligence crime is compatible with the normative imputation, both of which use the violation of norm as theoretical basis. In this regard, the normative imputation is the ideal model of imputation for negligence crime. In other words, normative imputation is ideal for attributing responsibility for the negligence crime.

3.3.2 Prerequisites for Normative Imputation to Deal with the Imputation Gap

According to the conclusion of the argument above, although the normative imputation is ideal imputation structure for negligence crime involving AI, the shift to normative imputation is not a complete rejection and abandonment of the will imputation. In fact, the typological thinking about facts and norms in the will imputation is also inherited by the normative imputation. In this sense, the relationship between these two kinds of imputation is not antagonistic, but rather inherited and developed. Therefore, in dealing with the gaps in the imputation for negligence crime involving AI, this shift in the imputation structure still requires adherence to the principle of self-responsibility formed in the will imputation structure [128, 129].

In addition, the typological thinking of distinguishing between factual description and normative evaluation, which is maintained by the will imputation, suggests that elements at the factual level do not have direct access to the scope of normative evaluation, and that they do not generally have normative judgment value at the normative level [130, 131]. Therefore, the first prerequisite for the normative imputation to deal with such imputation gap is to adhere to the principle of self-responsibility and typological thinking in the will imputation structure.

In the will imputation structure, there is no substantial difference in imputation between intentional and negligent crimes, since the basis for the imputation is the will of the perpetrator. In the case of negligence crime, the will-based imputation structure of intentional crimes applies directly to the negligence crime. However, the negligence crime does not in fact have the reason to condemn on the will, so the imputation for it can only take the possibility of foreseeing as the center of the criminal imputation. In this regard, it should be noted that, since the criminal law provides a relatively precise description and illustration of the intentional crimes in its constituent elements, such kind of relatively closed constituent element clarifies the scope of punishment and imputation for the intentional crimes [132, 133]. However, for the negligence crime, the criminal law does not clearly describe its constituent elements, but roughly describe them by citing a large number of norms in the corresponding fields. This determines that the constituent elements of negligence crime are open, unclear and need further explanation according to the traditional theory of the negligence crime [134, 135]. Therefore, in order to adapt to the shift towards the normative imputation with the base of norm violation, the constituent elements of the negligence crime need to describe the breach of the duty of care in as much detail as possible. Therefore, the establishment of the constituent elements of the negligence crime, and thus the substantiation of it in the negligence crime, is the key to the shift of the normative imputation structure of such crime.

In order to meet the need for the shift in the imputation structure of negligence crime to normative imputation, it is necessary to supplement the constituent elements of such crime through the objective imputation theory, so as to realize the substantivity of the constituent elements for the negligence crime [136, 137]. In this way, the theory of objective imputation provides the basis for the judgment of what constitutes the negligence crime, including its basic concepts and the content and steps for the judgment of constituent elements. For example, the act creates and realizes a risk that is not permitted by the law, and the corresponding result is realized within the scope of protection of the norm. As for the imputation for the negligence crime, its various imputation problems caused by using the foreseeability of the perpetrator as the basis for its judgment can thus be avoided [121, 124]. According to the previous arguments, the objective imputation theory has been developed by Pufendorf, Larenz, Honig, Roxin, and others, and it has demonstrated strong theoretical advantages in determining the fulfillment of the constitutive elements of crimes.

According to the above discussion, the imputation structure of negligence crime should shift from will imputation to normative imputation. This shift not only alleviates the impact of the application of AI on the traditional theory of imputation for the negligence crime, thus avoiding the gap in the imputation for such crime, but also facilitates the improvement of the theory of the constituent elements as well as of the unlawfulness in the negligence crime. As far as the constituent elements of negligence crimes are concerned, since the normative imputation structure has incorporated the normative evaluation into the judgment of fulfillment of the constituent elements, this compensates for the shortcomings of factual causation and thus achieves a reasonable limitation of the scope of the liability [57, 138]. In addition, the normative imputation theory shifts the focus of judgment on the fulfillment of constituent elements from the subjective elements to objective ones, which greatly reduces the significance of the subjective constituent elements in this judgment, and thus making this judgment more reasonable [36, 139].

Moreover, the significance of this shift to the normative imputation is also reflected in the theory of unlawfulness in the negligence crime. To a certain extent, the objective imputation theory has restructured the system of unlawfulness in the negligence crime [111, 140, 141]. According to the verification of objective imputation, as long as the result of the unlawfulness of the negligence can be attributed to the perpetrator, the act is bound to constitute the crime of negligence [96, 107]. In that case, the judgment of some so-called key concepts in the traditional theory of negligence crime, such as the violation of the duty of care, the foreseeability, the possibility of recognizing and avoiding, etc., have no significance in the constitute of the negligence crime. As a result, the realization of the shift in the normative imputation for the negligence crime means not only the change in the imputation structure, but also this shift directly leads to the redefinition of the unlawfulness of negligence crimes. It is the issues that are faced in the imputation for negligence crime involving AI. Therefore, the shift in the imputation structure o to the normative imputation is of great significance in addressing the challenges to imputation for the negligence crime.

3.4 Verification in the Normative Imputation for Negligence Crime Involving AI

The challenges brought by the development and application of AI to the crimes involving AI are mainly centered on the emergence of imputation gaps in the negligence crime involving AI. According to the conclusion of the previous argument, the main reason for this gap is that the traditional will imputation structure and the constituent elements of the negligence crime are over-reliance on the subjective element of such negligence crime. In order to address these gaps in the criminal imputation, the shift in the imputation structure from will imputation to normative imputation is a rational choice. In addition, the objective imputation theory has already provided a verification basis for this shift in the normative imputation structure. However, how can we conduct these verifications in the imputation for negligence crime involving AI? This is undoubtedly the core of the imputation theory for the negligence crime involving AI.

3.4.1 Verification of the Permitted Risk

In the theory of objective imputation, the prerequisite for the imputation verification is that the act creates the risk that are not permitted by law [97, 142]. In this sense, such risk gives the normative evaluation to the factual elements of actus reus, so it itself is a normative description of the state of act and result. In this way, risk can be understood as a normatively evaluated state of affairs in which the act may trigger the realization of a result.

Risks Posed by AI and Permitted by Criminal Law

The Risk, in general, is the risk that is not permitted by the norms of criminal law. However, the question is, is risk, so understood, the risk in the imputation for negligence crime involving AI? The answer to this question is the key to the shift of the imputation theory for negligence crime in order to meet the challenge of criminal imputation brought about by the criminal risks of AI. Generally speaking, the risk associated with AI is both the technological risks that causes the occurrence of crime involving AI, and the risks of gaps in the imputation for negligence crime involving AI.

In fact, the consistency between the risk brought by AI and the risks not allowed by law is mainly reflected in the following aspects. Firstly, in both types of risk, act and its corresponding result are the common focus. In the context of permitted risk, risk refers to the danger of consequences caused by the behavior of the offender. Therefore, the most basic condition for giving risk normative value is the human subjectivity [96, 110]. In other words, the object evaluated by risk is the behavior and its result. In the normative sense of criminal law, no matter how the theory of act is defined, human beings are regarded as the only subjects of act. According to the conclusion in the previous argument, the subject of crimes involving AI is still a natural person. This natural person-centered idea has not yet been broken through in the concept of AI. Therefore, whether it is AI technology or the crimes involving AI, the object of the normative evaluation is always the natural person, i.e., the act and its result of the natural person.

Secondly, the most important significance of risk in the context of permitted risk is that it assigns the evaluative value to behaviors and outcomes in the normative sense, thus providing the possibility for the act and its result to be evaluated by the criminal law norm. In addition to promoting social progress, the development and application of AI technology may also lead to the occurrence of crimes involving AI, thereby threatening not only the social public order but also the security of the legal interests of citizen. Therefore, in order to effectively deal with this kind of risk, it needs to accept the normative evaluation of criminal law [143, 144]. In this sense, both types of risks have the significance of normative evaluation from criminal law. Finally, both risks involve the judgment as to whether is permitted or not. Generally speaking, risk manifests itself as a neutral fact in its original state, but its nature needs to be determined after a normative evaluation. For AI, the risk brought about by the development and application of its technology is the inevitable costs and payments for the social development, because society will lose its ability to move forward without such risks [145, 146].

However, on the other hand, such kind of risk may jeopardize the social order and the legal interests of citizens. Therefore, the ideal state is to maintain a reasonable balance between such two kinds of risk. If the risk posed by the development and application of AI breaks the above balance, it will inevitably lead to a negative evaluation by the criminal law. However, if such a risk is limited to a certain extent, the risk may be permissible by the criminal law [147, 148]. What is crucial here is how to strike a reasonable balance between the two kinds of risks. It can be seen that the permitted risk is consistent with the risk caused by the development and application of AI, which suggests that the theory of permitted risk provides a feasible way to address the issue of imputation for the negligence crime involving AI.

Risk Involving AI and Its Determination

According to the common understanding of criminal law theory, permitted risk means that the perpetrator complies with the corresponding legal provisions when committing an act that carries a certain level of risk. Then, the behavior is a permitted risk behavior within the scope of the risk that the law can tolerate. Consequently, the behavior cannot fulfill the constituent elements of the crime because it does not infringe upon the legal interests [149, 150]. It follows that the risk permitted by the law can be understood from both the legislative and judicial aspects.

In practice, certain behaviors that are beneficial to society are often accompanied by certain risk. However, if this risk should be more affirmed in terms of benefit compared with the promotion of social development by this behavior, then the law should allow the existence of behavior with this kind of risk. In this regard, we should understand this risk as a legally significant risk created by the actor, so this risk is permissible. For example, the clinical trial is sometimes risky to our life and health, but the legislator still allows such risky behavior. Therefore, if the perpetrator complies with the relevant laws and regulations, the normal conduct of clinical trial is a risky behavior permitted by the law [151, 152]. For another example, although the road traffic poses certain risks to human life, health and property, the legislator still allows for such kind of risks. Therefore, someone drives his car in compliance with the corresponding road traffic rules is a risky behavior allowed by the law. As long as certain behaviors are conducive to the development and progress of our society, the law should allow for the existence of these risks within certain limits. For such risks, it involves the considerations from the legislative aspect.

At the legislative aspect, the main consideration of risks is whether certain risks are legally permissible through the legislation. In addition to this, whether the behavior is with the permitted risk is to consider whether to fulfill the constituent elements of some specific crime from the judicial aspect [153, 154]. In other words, if the behavior of the perpetrator meets the demands of the permitted risk by law, the behavior does not fulfill the constituent elements of some specific crime because it has not infringed any legal interest. This kind of permitted risk at the judicial level is generally based on the value choice and institutional construction at the legislative level. For example, though the legislation, the permitted risk is given some certain limitation, and the behavior is only permitted with no prohibited risk if it meets those conditions. In most cases, the legislator generally requires that the perpetrator must be careful to take certain obligations in order to make the risk of his behavior legally permitted [155, 156]. In judicial practice, this kind of stipulation is often the basis for deciding whether the behavior of the perpetrator is with permitted risk.

Despite these legal requirements, the question is, on what criteria can we judge and decide these permitted risks? According to the previous discussion, the risk of an act is permitted only because it is beneficial to society. Therefore, according to some views, the benefit to society is also a criterion for determining whether a risk is permissible [76, 157]. However, what is the significance of this abstract socially beneficial standard for the unlawfulness of the negligence crime? In fact, the specific scope of duty of care from the perpetrator cannot be determined with such abstract standard of the social benefit [158, 159]. In this regard, a premise that needs to be determined is that the criteria for deciding the permitted risk should be different with its different purposes. The previously discussed criterion of benefit to society, that is, the interest balance, can be considered at the abstract legislative stage as well as at the specific judicial application stage. Accordingly, this can be discussed in the following abstract and specific ways.

Firstly, the criterion for judging the permitted risk is expressed at the legislative level as an abstract benefit weight, which is determined by the attributes of the legislative activity [160, 161]. From a long-term and macro perspective, the risk of an act is permitted at the stage of legislation if it can promote the social progress and public well-being, and the risk it poses is controllable within certain limits.

Therefore, after comprehensively balancing the various existing interests in society with the interests that may arise in the future, the legislator places the balanced interests of all parties in a specific legal system, thus he has completed the interest balance at the legislative level [162, 163].

Secondly, the specific criterion for determining the permitted risk derives from the specific judicial practice. In the specific judicial application, to determine such criterion must meet the following principal requirements: First, because the interest weight at the stage of legislation has priority, the corresponding criterion at the stage of judicial application should be consistent with it at the stage of legislation in the value orientation [164, 165]. That is to say, the criterion in judicial practice is in fact the specific application of the legislative criterion, and the conclusions drawn by the two in practice should be consistent with each other, Second, the judicial practice should not only realize the actual interest weight, but also to ensure the realization of the efficient judicial practice. Therefore, in judicial practice, various duties of care stipulated by legislator are often used as criterion for deciding whether the risks are permitted in the criminal law [166, 167]. In this case, since the legislator has stipulated the socially beneficial behavior in the form of various specific norms of care, we can judge whether the corresponding risk is permitted by law depending on whether or not the perpetrator has violated the duty of care.

The question is, however, how should the norms of criminal law determine the duty of care if there are no corresponding laws, regulations, industry guidelines, etc., in such emerging fields as AI? If there is no such defined duty, how to determine whether the risk implied by the behavior is permissible under the law? In this regard, the substantive criterion of the permitted risk can provide a basis for such risk determination by overcoming the shortcomings and deficiencies of the criterion at the legislative stage. The substantive criterion in the judicial practice means that the nature of permitted risk is determined by the nature of duty of care, which is the basis for determining whether the risk is permissible or not [156, 168]. In the field of AI, although its development and application has greatly contributed to the social development and public well-being, the uncertainty of its technology has posed many new challenges to the law and social ethics. In the practice, there have been numerous violations and crimes involving AI, which also illustrates that it is a science and technology accompanied by significant risks [169–171].

Therefore, in the face of the opportunities and challenges posed by the development and application of AI, the law must make value judgments and trade-offs. In fact, the risk derived from AI technology is the inevitable and reasonable cost for the social progress and public welfare. With regard to such risk, criminal law norms should determine which risks involving AI break through the value bias of interest balance and are prohibited by law, and determine whether the risks derived from the relevant behaviors are permissible under criminal law by stipulating the duty of care.

Permitted Risk and Imputation for Negligence Crime Involving AI

According to the previous conclusion, the theory of objective imputation is of decisive significance in dealing with the gaps in the imputation for the negligence crime involving AI, thus realizing the shift of the imputation structure from will to normative imputation. Therefore, after making the judgment on whether the risk arising from the development and application of AI are permitted or not, there is still a need to discuss the significance of such permitted risk for the imputation for the negligence crime involving AI.

In contrast to will imputation, the normative imputation takes the violation of norm by the behavior as its basis for attributing the responsibility. The fundamental reason why the two elements of behavior and norm can be evaluated in the normative imputation structure is that the normative imputation requires the evaluation of the normative value of the behavior [172, 173]. In line with this, it is precisely the requirement of permitted risk in the normative imputation structure that provides the possibility for the behavior to accept its normative evaluation, since the theory of permitted risk is in fact aims at normative evaluation of risk brought about by the behavior. In the normative imputation, behavior has the possibility of normative evaluation only if it has the important legal significance.

Thus, the risk in the sense of permitted risk is the evaluation of the normative value that the act has. In practice, if the behavior does not create a risk that is not permitted by the law, then the behavior is not the behavior with risk in the sense of imputation, and the behavior has not possibility to fulfill the constitutive elements of crime [174, 175]. In this sense, it can be affirmed that various daily behaviors are common in life and do not bring about the legal risks. Even if these have certain results, they do not fulfill the constitutive elements of a crime only because they not only involve the risk prohibited by law. It follows that the theory of permitted risk in fact gives the normative value to the risk brought about by the development and application of AI technology.

In the case of AI technology, both its development and application may involve some specific crime. For example, negligence crimes can often be found in the different circumstances during the design, production and application of AI technology [170, 176, 177]. The only way to make a decision on whether or not the behavior should be attributed to a risk derived from AI technologies is to evaluate whether it is a risk prohibited by the criminal law. It is only with this normative evaluation of such risks derived from AI technology that their nature can realize their transition from the factual to the normative level. At the same time, the criterion of permitted risk at the legislative stage can also indicate the existence of the legal risk involving AI. For example, the judgment on whether the open AI such as ChatGPT poses risks in the areas such as the social life, health, transportation, education, etc., can be obtained through criterion at the legislative level as to whether these risks are permissible under the law. In practice, the law regulates and evaluates any risk by establishing the corresponding prudential rules [178, 179]. For example, the application of autopilot technology and the development of competitive sports all prove the existence of legally significant risks through the standardization of the corresponding safety precautions. This suggests that the legally significant risks of AI technology have the value and possibility of normative evaluation.

However, not all such kind of legally significant risk should be negatively evaluated by the law norms, as some risks may still be permitted by norms after balancing the corresponding interests. For this kind of risk, criminal law sets a certain duty of care to exclude the behaviors that meet the requirements of such duty from the scope of its normative evaluation. In this way, criminal law determines the risks it allows [180, 181]. Today, with the increase of risks in society, criminal law as a whole is becoming more and more oriented towards its preventive function. Accordingly, the criterion for judging the risk in criminal law norms has been gradually lowered, thus realizing the earlier and more risks to be regulated by the criminal law.

In the context of criminal law, the prohibited risk holds significant importance due to its reliance on the duty of care. This aspect becomes particularly crucial in the imputation for negligence crime involving AI, where the comprehensive laws, regulations, and industry standards are still in the process of being established and refined. Indeed, the absence of duty of care is precisely what gives rise to the gaps of criminal imputation [2, 182]. Consequently, the permitted risk assessment liberates such imputation from excessive reliance on such formal judgment standards to some extent.

3.4.2 *Behavior with Creating Prohibited Risk*

The determination of the permitted risk has opened up the possibility of avoiding the imputation gaps caused by over-reliance on the duty of care in the imputation for negligence crime involving AI. However, the attribution of a result to the perpetrator still needs to establish that the result is the realization of a prohibited risk created by the perpetrator. Only then should the perpetrator be held liable for that result. Thus, determining that the perpetrator has created a legally impermissible risk is an important step in the normative imputation for the negligence crime involving AI. In this regard, how to verify that the perpetrator created a prohibited risk is the main content of the next argument.

Risk Responsibility

For crimes, there is no difference in their nature in that the perpetrator ignores the requirements of the law and order to participate in maintaining the existing state of freedom [183]. Thus, there are no general crime, only specific, concrete crime. The understanding of crime can only acquire its necessary contours by reference to the concrete embodiment of freedom in others, and the protection of freedom is to a certain extent the duty of one person [84]. A key concept here, therefore, is the responsibility of the perpetrator. Why is the perpetrator required to take into account the integrity of the interests of others when he commits his acts? And to what extent is he obliged to take this into account? In fact, these questions arise in the same way in each of the constitutive elements of crime. Consequently, criminal law has long sought to concretize and systematize the various elements of responsibility [84].

The fundamental aim of law, especially criminal law, is that citizens can live their own lives according to their own judgment. To do this, they must be able to rely on the integrity of the law for their rights to be respected by others. However, criminal law may also, to a certain extent, require citizens to make a certain contribution to the maintenance of the functioning of the State. It follows that the task of criminal law is to ensure the freedom of citizens on the one hand and the normal operation of the country on the other. From such tasks of the criminal law, we can obtain the legitimate basis for the responsibility of citizen. In fact, every citizen will not bear a responsibility that is unfoundedly imposed on him [184]. To some extent, the responsibility of each citizen is to ensure the survival of the individual. However, the question is, how are the responsibilities of each individual to be distributed in their social life?

Different from the will imputation, which is based on the foreseeability, the normative imputation takes the responsibility allocation of the actor as an important theoretical basis for its imputation [185, 186]. It is generally believed that people can usually understand the course and results of things, and can effectively control the things they know. In the criminal law, this conception affects the constitutive elements of the negligence crime and the allocation of responsibility. According to this understanding, what person has at his dominance can only be something with the predictable probability, and this probability implies the possibility of the domination by the perpetrator. In fact, domination means taking the responsibility. Therefore, in order for the perpetrator to be held responsible for the specific results, the premise can only be that he has the possibility of foreseeing this result, otherwise it would be contrary to the basic principle of responsibility [187–189]. Affected by this, the key to imputation for the negligence crime is the possibility of the perpetrator foreseeing the outcome. However, with the leapfrog development and application of science and technology, especially AI, the resulting uncertainty far exceeds the cognitive ability of the most people, which leads to a challenge to the traditional judgment of the foreseeability in the negligence crime. In this regard, people may generally be able to foresee the abstract dangers, but they may be generally unable to foresee the concrete dangers.

Indeed, as risk becomes increasingly pervasive and uncertain, the traditional imputation structure focusing on the foreseeability is unable to effectively deal with the gaps in the imputation for the negligence crime involving AI. The main reason here is that the foreseeable possibility of an outcome does not necessarily equate to the possibility of dominating such outcome [190, 191]. Therefore, the principle upheld by the traditional theory of negligence crime is that the person who has foresight or the possibility of foreseeing the risk should be responsible for the results caused by the risk. In fact, this result of such imputation constructure is increasingly divorced from the reality of the social development today. This difficulty in the imputation, caused by the inconsistency between the foreseeability and domination in the practice, has prompted the theory to identify a new element to achieve a normative link with the possibility of domination. Moreover, since the domination may imply the assumption of the responsibility, such new element is at the same time the basis for the allocation of the responsibility [38, 137]. In this context, the doctrine of risk responsibility comes out.

In the social communication, everyone has an obligation to ensure that his behavior do not bring harm to the interests of others, and therefore he needs to be responsible for his behavior. Accordingly, the perpetrator must be held responsible for the risks posed by his behavior. In this context, the so-called risk responsibility means that the person to whom the risk belongs is responsible for the risk and its results [192, 193]. That is, anyone who has dominion over the occurrence of a fact, he must be held responsible for the occurrence of the fact. According to this principle, everyone must arrange well his own activity space, and he must not export any danger to his own space that can threaten the interests of others, otherwise he will bear responsibility for his behavior [194, 195]. Specifically in the case of negligence crime, the risk responsibility is the basis for the imputation.

Therefore, the attribution of the result to the perpetrator needs to be determined by examining whether the perpetrator exercised reasonable management of the risk within his responsibility, in addition to identifying whose responsibility the risk falls within. What can be ascertained from the foregoing discussion is that risk responsibility effectively replaces the role of the foreseeability in the imputation for the negligence crime, thus arguing for the imputation by domination over the risk.

Boundary of Risk Responsibility

As Kant explained in a lecture on moral philosophy, only those consequences that flow from the freedom of the actor can be imputed [196]. This kind of freedom is lacking, on the one hand, in the conduct of those who are not capable of imputation, such as the behavior of child, and, on the other hand, in unavoidable events, such as the necessity. In these cases, the actor was unable to prevent these events from occurring, either because they were beyond the capacity of the human being or because he could not have foreseen their occurrence of such events. This rule applies in all such cases, and no one is liable for anything beyond his competence [196].

If the actor is inevitably wrong about what he is required, or he is unreasonably anticipated not to act contrary to his ability to dominate the risks, then he should not be held responsible for the results of his behavior. This is a consideration of the possibility to attribute the responsibility to the perpetrator from the point of view of freedom, that is to say, the perpetrator must be able to refrain from committing behaviors that are incompatible with his risk responsibility capacity [197, 198]. It follows that the risk responsibility boundary is decisive in determining whether or not the perpetrator is responsible for his own behavior.

Nowadays, with the extensive development and application of AI technology, the social activities involving AI are becoming increasingly complex compared to the traditional social activities. In the design, production, and application of AI, the complexity of AI technology has resulted in a fragmented and intertwined field of risk responsibility for the relevant participants [199, 200]. This complexity, however, is not the reason to prevent the establishment of a clear boundary of the risk responsibility for the perpetrator involving AI. Compared with the traditional abstract judgment on the possibility of foreseeability in the negligence crime, the determination of this boundary is at least objectively determinable. In this regard, for the division and determination of the boundary of risk responsibility involving AI, there stand two theoretical views that attempt to make a clear definition of such boundary between the AI-related participants, including AI designers, producers and users.

To this end, one view is based on the theory of dominance obligations. According to this point, it is argued that the judgment of risk domination in the scenarios involving AI equate to the violation of domination obligations [201, 202]. As far as the theory of crime domination is concerned, Welzel explained all the crimes except the negligence crime in a unified way by the crime domination over the social facts [203]. In contrast, Roxin divides the principal offenders into the dominant offenders, compulsory offenders and hands-on offenders according to the different constituent elements of crimes [204, 205]. According to his understanding, the principal offender is the person, who dominates the corpus delicti, while the compulsory offender does not dominate the corpus delicti, but he violates the special obligations from the specific constituent elements of the crime. Since the domination over the corpus delicti has the room only for the application in the domination offenses, corpus delicti domination cannot explain all types of the principal offenses.

Schünemann, however, advocates a theory of normative domination over the corpus delicti domination, whereby he unites dominant and obligatory offender under the principle of normative domination over the corpus delicti [206]. According to his understanding, the domination is domination over events in the sense of social control. Consistent with this, Murmann understands the domination as control over the nature of the relationships [207]. It follows from this that all of these different views consider the domination over the corpus delicti to be the normative standard of the judgment, which contains special subjective and objective constituent elements, and therefore the domination theory applies to all kinds of crimes.

It follows that this domination theory advocates that the person with domination obligations regards the area in which it has obligations as the scope of his risk responsibility. Moreover, in this case, the setting of domination obligations for the perpetrator is based on the principal model of the traditional social activities. This means that when a natural person uses AI to take a certain activity, the natural person shall be obliged to dominate the activity of the AI if he acts as the subject who dominates the course of the whole activity [208–210]. In cases where the AI produces a harmful result, according to the theory, it should be considered to be the result of the conduct of the natural person and be attributed to the perpetrator. For example, even if a car is Full Self-Driving, the natural person driver should still take the obligation of dominance over the car during the self-driving process [211, 212].

In contrast to this view, which determines risk responsibility on the basis of the traditional social behavior, another view holds that the obligation of a natural person to dominate the events should be determined on the actual circumstances in activities involving AI [61, 213]. According to this understanding, the AI undeniably has a certain force in the overall development of the events. Objectively, it is the behavior of the natural person together with the AI that cause a certain result to occur. In the Full Self-Driving, where is the boundary of risk responsibility for the perpetrator? According to this view, such boundary should ultimately determine whether the perpetrator violated his duty of care [214, 215]. In addition, in order to bridge the gaps in the imputation, it should be confirmed that the natural person driver's duty of care should also be reduced while the Full Self-Driving vehicle continues to operate normally. It can be seen that this view equates the judgment of risk responsibility with the breach of the duty of care [215, 216]. It does not simply attribute the risk responsibility to a particular subject, but rather advocates a specific judgment based on a specific situation.

The key to the discussion here is how to draw the boundaries of risk responsibility of the natural person in cases where AI is involved in the behavior of this natural person. Compared with the view of determining this boundary through the obligation to dominate the traditional social activities, it is more reasonable to specifically determine such boundary of the involved natural person on the basis of the circumstances and extent of the AI involvement. This is because it takes into account the new features of the social activity in situations where AI is involved. When confronted with an increasingly intertwined field of risk responsibility, this view of concrete analysis based on the specific situations is more feasible and accurate. For example, in the field of automatic drive, driving automation functions are categorized into 6 different levels from 0 to 5 depending on the driving tasks that the driving automation system can perform. Among them, Levels 0–2 are collectively referred to as "Driving Assistance", which is a low-level automatic drive function, and Levels 3–5 are collectively referred to as "Automated Driving". This category into the different levels is based on the degree to which the automatic drive system is able to perform dynamic driving tasks, and on the assignment of roles in performing the dynamic driving tasks [217, 218]. Accordingly, levels 0–5 are: 0: emergency assistance; 1: partial driver assistance; 2: combined driver assistance; 3: conditionally automated driving; 4: highly automated driving; 5: fully automated driving.

On this premise, what is decisive for the automated drive are driving maneuvers, driving environment monitoring and failure response. In this regard, it has been argued that risk responsibility of the driver in the driving course of the self-driving cars can be divided into three areas accordingly [219, 220]. As drivers undertake different driving tasks in the different autonomous driving levels, the scope of their risk responsibility should also vary. For example, in the level of partial driver assistance, the risk responsibility boundary of the driver should include the driving operations that must be completed by the driver, driving environment monitoring, and failure response. If a risk occurs during this level of driving, then the risk falls within the risk responsibility boundary of the driver, and he has the possibility of being held responsible for this risk [219, 221]. In the level of conditionally automated driving, since the driving system completes all driving operations, the driver can only take over the driving at any time according to the prompts of the driving system. Therefore, in such level, the risk to the driver only occurs in the course of the failure response.

In this case, only when the risk occurs when the driver takes over the driving, the risk can fall within the risk responsibility boundary of the driver.

It follows that drivers have different boundaries of risk responsibility at the different levels of the automatic drive. From this example, it can be found that the key to determining whether a perpetrator has created a prohibited risk is to determine the boundary of risk responsibility of him. Only when the risk occurs within the boundary of the risk responsibility of the perpetrator, he has the possibility of imputation and the need for the further judgment.

Created Prohibited Risks by Breach of Duty of Care

In the light of the previous discussion and conclusions, the prohibited risk created by the perpetrator can only be those within the boundary of his risk responsibility. This kind of risk opens up the possibility of attributing the responsibility to the perpetrator. However, the question is, in the imputation for the negligence crime involving AI, how to determine that the perpetrator has created the risk within the boundary of his risk responsibility that are prohibited by law?

Generally, whenever the perpetrator in the negligence crime breaches his duty of care, his behavior has created a prohibited risk. Therefore, whether the perpetrator violates his duty of care is the key to deciding whether his behavior creates the prohibited risk in the negligence crime [70, 71, 222, 223]. Unlike the civil purposes such as compensation for damages and reinstatement, the fundamental purpose of criminal law is not to protect the legal interests as the generally understood, but to ensure the norm validity of criminal law [12, 224, 225]. To this end, criminal law requires not only that the citizen must ensure that he can avoid violating the norm if he has the actual capacity of complying with it, but also that he should ensure that he has the necessary capabilities to comply with the norm, thus preventing his corresponding capabilities inappropriate degradation. When the perpetrator in the negligence crime commits his behavior, although he does not intend to violate the norms of the law, he causes the result to occur only because of his own carelessness, and therefore the result can still be attributed to the perpetrator [226, 227].

It follows that it is precisely because the perpetrator improperly reduces his ability to comply with the norms that his behavior creates a risk prohibited by the law, which is a prerequisite for the illegality of act in the negligence crime. The standard, which is used to determine whether the perpetrator has improperly reduced his capacity to act, is whether the actor has violated his duty of care [228–230]. Indeed, the duty of care is a capacity that maintains the ability of the perpetrator to comply with the norm. If he breaches his duty of care, this unduly reduces his own capacity to comply with the norm. In this case, his breach of the duty of care means, in effect, that he has created a risk of violating the legal norm and thereby damages the validity of the norm [37, 66]. As for whether the risk occurs in reality, this is completely beyond the control of the perpetrator, and that is the prohibited risk created by his behavior. The question is, however, what duty of care was breached by the perpetrator in his creating such prohibited risk?

In the case of negligence crime involving AI, the subjects in such crime are the designers, producers and users of AI. Since their duty of care is not explicit in the norms, what is crucial for the imputation is to determine what kind of duty of care has been breached by the corresponding actor. The key question here is, where do these duties come from? In this regard, there is a great deal of controversy either in theory or in practice, as the content and scope of the duty of the care is not clearly defined in the law. For example, it has been argued that industry standards are the source of the duty and that the scope of the duty of care is therefore limited to the national or industry standards that are within the reach of the current development state of science and technology [231, 232]. Other views, however, argue that industry standards are not a duty of care under criminal law, and therefore argue that statutory obligations created by the State are the legitimate source of the duty [233–235]. The view was also expressed that laws and regulations, industry standards, self-commitment of the responsible person, general social ethics, professional ethics, etc., should all be sources of the duty of care [236, 237].

Although there is no theoretical consensus on the source of the duty of care, the industry standard is relatively the reasonable source of such a duty. In the case of negligence crime involving AI, a relatively strict duty of care should be imposed on the designers and producers of AI, as this will help to ensure the validity of norm in the criminal law [238, 239]. In addition, regulated industry standards are not in conflict with the statutory and social obligations, as they are regulated according to the laws and regulations and must also comply with the requirements of the social obligations. In fact, these industry standards should place higher professional and technical requirements on the designers and producers in such professional fields as AI, because these technical requirements are often beyond the reach of laws and ethics [240, 241]. In terms of the feasibility of judging such duty of care, the industry standard is likewise the most reasonable choice as a source of duty of care. Compared with the most principal normative content of laws, regulations and social ethics, such industry standards can more comprehensively and specifically stipulate the duty of care of AI designers, producers and users [3, 209, 242]. In practice, when specifically judging this duty of care of the perpetrator, the detailed and specific industry standards are the guarantee of such accurate judgment.

However, since the provisions of professional negligence crime in the criminal law are based much more on the provisions of the relevant administrative regulations, these industry standards are not explicitly stipulated in the constituent elements of negligence crime, and the duty of care of the perpetrator is determined by the blank facts about a crime. The question here is, how to determine these duties of care based on those relevant administrative regulations? For the professional negligence crime, the use of the corresponding administrative regulations to supplement their blank facts of the offenses is decisive in determining the perpetrator's duty of care [243–245]. This is because the corresponding statutory norms, such as laws, statutes, and regulations, used to supplement the blank facts of such offenses can both typologically infer the duty of care and delineate the boundaries of prohibited risk.

However, the ability of the specific perpetrator to foresee and avoid something still remains an inseparable and foundational criterion for judging the breach of the duty of care in the case of professional negligence crime [246, 247]. Specifically, this kind of norm that fills in the blank facts of the crime has the following significance in judging the duty of care: firstly, in order to cope with the risks associated with the development and application of AI technology, the country and industry will set up the protective laws and industry regulations for the entire process from research to application of AI technology is to control this risk within the controllable and minimum limit. For the perpetrator, once he has consciously violated such relevant norms, it can be inferred that he is responsible for the reduction in his ability to foresee and avoid something. It follows that the breach of the duty of care by the perpetrator can be established on the basis of such filler norms that the perpetrator has breached. Secondly, for the perpetrator, if he carefully complies with the norms that fill in the blank facts of the crime, then the occurrence of the harmful result is a permissible risk that is not attributable to him. In this way, such norms formally define the boundary of the permitted risk [226, 248].

As previously discussed, since the norms that fill the blank facts of the negligence crime are capable of typologically inferring the duty of care, it is possible to determine what kind of duty of care has been violated whenever the perpetrator violates those norms. However, whether the behavior of the perpetrator thereby has created a risk prohibited by law still requires a substantive determination of whether he has reduced his ability to foresee something due to his violating these norms.

Ground for Elimination of Creation of Prohibited Risk

The fact that the behavior has created a risk prohibited by law means that there is no ground for elimination of creating of the prohibited risk. Only when the behavior does not have such ground for the elimination can it be determined that the behavior creates the risk that are not permitted by law. Thus, this kind of ground is critical to determining whether the behavior has created a risk prohibited by law.

According to such elimination grounds, the risks created by the actor are excluded from the scope of risks that are not permitted by law, and there is no possibility of the actor being attributed for the risk for his behavior. Specifically, when the actor performs the behavior, which lacks risk prohibited by law in the practice [249, 250]. This is one of the grounds for the elimination. In this case, even though the actor does not reduce a risk of damage to the norm validity, but also does not increase this risk in a legally noteworthy way, then his behavior excludes that it has created the risk that is not permitted by law [251, 252]. By its nature, the behavior of the perpetrator belongs to the daily life activity that has no legal significance. Thus, even if such behavior is capable of leading to some harmful consequences in the rare and exceptional circumstances, the risk is minimal in terms of social appropriateness and should therefore be ignored by the law [150, 253].

In this case, the risks created by the daily behavior of the perpetrator are not of concern to the law. In other words, only because such behavior has not created a risk worthy of legal evaluation from the outset, so the risk should be eliminated from the category of the prohibited risk. A common example of this in the literature is that the nephew who wanted to inherit the property from his uncle and persuaded him to go for a walk in the forest, expecting that his uncle would be struck by the lightning and die during his walk. It turned out that his uncle was indeed struck by lightning and died during his walking. In that example, the behavior in persuading the uncle to take a walk did not create any risk worthy of the legal evaluation, and therefore could not be attributed to the actor because of the unintended consequences.

As long as the behavior creates risk that has no legal significance, it will be excluded from the scope of the prohibited risk. In addition, behavior that has reduced the associated risk is also a ground for elimination of creation of prohibited risk [109, 254]. When the perpetrator reduces from the outset the risk that already existed by the victim, the possibility of attributing the risk created by the perpetrator is excluded on this ground. In this case, when the perpetrator in fact interferes with the development of a causal process in the way that improves the condition of the object of the act, the prohibited risk created by him is not eliminated [88, 89]. For example, a falling tree trunk falls from the top of a hill and is about to hit tourist A. At that moment, B pushes A backward. As a result, the tree trunk would have hit the head of A and this would have caused his death with a high probability, but due to behavior of B, the tree trunk finally hit him on the shoulder and injured one of his shoulders. In this example, although there is a causal connection between the result of A's shoulder injury and B's behavior of pushing A backward, B's behavior does not create a risk that is not permitted by law. It is precisely because B's behavior actually reduces the risk that A would otherwise encounter that it eliminates the creation of a risk prohibited by law. This ground for elimination of prohibited risk is the risk reduction.

A related question is whether an actor creates a risk that is not permitted by law if he tries to mitigate an existing risk by creating a new risk. This is the theory of risk modification [255]. In a classic case that is often discussed, the father of a baby dropped his baby from a twenty-story building to prevent her from suffocating to death from the smoke of a burning flat. As a result, her daughter fell to the ground and died. In this case, a fact that cannot be ignored is that the baby was in danger of suffocating to death at any time by remaining in the room. Thus, although the risk of the outcome of the original elements of crime did not occur because of the intervention of the father's behavior, the father did therefore also create a new risk, which finally led to the death of the baby. In principle, the prohibitions or commandments of criminal law norms will not give up their own normative purposes and thus give up the protection of the legal interests of the victims just because the consequences are inevitable. This discussion has already dealt with the evaluation category of the preventing illegal emergency evacuation, which cannot be supported by objective imputation. In this sense, the assumption of causal processes cannot be used to exclude the imputation [256–258]. In this regard, the majority has argued that when the force majeure of nature intervenes, an exception can be made to the exclusion of the actor's attribution from the constitutive elements [88, 89].

According to the previous discussion, the constituent elements of professional negligence generally require other norms to fill in the blank facts of constituent elements. If the behavior fully complies with the requirements of these specifications, but still infringes the legal interests, does the behavior create risk that is prohibited by law? This deals with the ground for the elimination of prohibited risk. In this case, the main reason why such risk prohibited by law are excluded is that certain risk must be borne by the norms [158, 259]. In other words, if the perpetrator cannot avoid the occurrence of some specific risk while maintaining a normal level of care, then this risk should be excluded from the scope of risk that is not permitted by law. In essence, although the perpetrator violated the filled specifications, the specific content of the violation of such norms has nothing to do with the ability of the perpetrator to pay attention to something [99, 260]. Thus, the behavior did not actually reduce the capacity of the perpetrator to foresee and avoid, and therefore did not create a risk prohibited by law from the outset.

From the above discussion, it can be found that the risk created by the perpetrator is a legally impermissible risk only if he creates it within his own risk responsibility and such risk reduces his ability to comply with the norms, i.e., the ability to foresee and avoid the consequences. In other words, only the risk that actually results in an unreasonable reduction in the perpetrator's ability to foresee and avoid the consequences is this risk prohibited by law; otherwise, any risk created by him are excluded from the scope of their impermissibility by the legal order. From the logic of judgment, an act creates a risk prohibited by law as long as it does not have the ground for the elimination of creation of prohibited risk.

Created Prohibited Risk and Imputation for Negligence Crime Involving AI

The reason why the perpetrator has the possibility of being held liable for creating a risk that is not permitted by law is that the perpetrator has the obligation to ensure that there is no risk of harming the legal interests of others in the area where he dominates his risk responsibility. Therefore, the creation of risk prohibited by law is of great significance to the criminal imputation system. However, is the creation of risk equally of significant in the imputation for negligence crime involving AI?

Whether the negligence of perpetrator should be attributed to him or not, his foreseeability plays a decisive role in this decision. The judgment of such foreseeability is mainly based on the experience of people. In other words, this experience is the development law of the things and the objective existence of things that people acquire through practice [190, 191]. For the traditional negligence crime, it is reasonable to take this kind of foreseeability as the premise for the imputation. However, with the continuous development and wide application of AI technology, the ability of people to foresee the behavior and its results in activities involving AI is indeed greatly reduced. In practice, it is in fact difficult for man to accurately foresee the exact development direction of his behavior and the pattern of the outcomes in the situations of Human-in-the-Loop. In this case where AI is involved, the causality of some risks is extremely complex, so it is difficult for people to foresee the actual results of such risks. In addition, the experience is also insufficient to explain the mechanism and causal process of AI.

In this regard, according to the conclusion of the previous arguments, the imputation structure of negligence crime involving AI has shifted from the will imputation to the normative imputation. For this reason, more theories tend to determine the premise of imputation for such crime based on whether the behavior creates the prohibited risks, thereby trying to get rid of the limitations of foreseeability and reliance on the empirical facts. Therefore, the judgment of creation of prohibited risks is made with the base of norm [96, 261]. This normative nature is mainly reflected in the judgment of the created risk prohibited by law, because the risk must be created by the perpetrator in the boundary of his risk responsibility. Correspondingly, the confirmation of this boundary is based on the laws, regulations and industry norms of the industry in which the actor is located.

According to the common understanding of the negligence crime, the perpetrator can only control what he can foresee, and only what he can control can be attributed to him. Therefore, the factual relationship between his behavior and its result is the logical basis for the imputation for the negligence crime. In this kind of imputation, the factual causality still plays the role in linking the perpetrator, behavior, results and the imputation, thereby realizing that responsibility can be effectively attributed to the actor along the causal relationship [57, 262]. It can be seen that the causality in the traditional theory of imputation not only reaffirms the significance of foreseeability for the imputation, but also embodies the requirement of causality for such imputation. However, in the imputation for negligence crime involving AI, the determination of this causality is hindered by the complex operating mechanism of AI in the practice.

On this point, the theory of risk responsibility can effectively avoid this problem. As claimed to the principle of this theory, any person must organize his own space of activity so as to ensure that no danger to the interests of others is exported from this space of his activity [263, 264]. In this sense, identifying the causal flow of events in order to recognize the process of infringing a legal interest is no longer the content of the imputation, but rather determining to whom the duty to avoid infringing a legal interest belongs, or to whom the responsibility belongs, becomes the focus of the criminal imputation. Accordingly, the criminal imputation is no longer based on the criterion of the foreseeability. Thus, a person who creates a risk permitted by law will not be attributed liability even if he has a foreseeability of result, conversely, a person who creates a risk prohibited by law may be attributed liability even if he lacks the foreseeability of the specific result [50, 123].

This is not to suggest, however, that the factual causation is entirely irrelevant to the criminal imputation [265, 266]. According to the risk creation theory, if the behavior reduces the risk that would otherwise exist, then the attribution to the perpetrator is precluded. In this case, although there is such a factual causation between the risk-reducing behavior and the occurrence of the result, there is a normative limitation on the retroactive function of liability for this causation [39, 78, 267]. It is thus clear that the factual causation is not the only way in which the responsibility can be traced back to. The causation must be decided through the normative evaluation in order to penetrate the connection between the act and the result, between responsibility and the subject in the crime.

The development of science and technology has resulted in an increasingly detailed and complex division of labor in the traditional societies. This finally leads to the fact that people can only control the behavior within the area of his risk responsibility, but they are unable to control and dominate all the processes of industrial production [195, 268]. Especially with the rapid development and widespread application of AI technology, all the aspects of AI, including its design, production, and application, are interconnected and thus complement each other in the performance of its functions. Thus, in the event of a negligence crime involving AI, the attribution of responsibility to the perpetrators needs to determine the allocation of risk creation among the subjects of the crime at its different stages [3, 269, 270]. For this reason, the field of responsibility of each subject can only be determined by dividing the different fields of risk responsibility of them in accordance with the theory of risk responsibility.

When the risk is realized in the practice, the field of risk responsibility for which each subject should be responsible can really play a role in determining the scope of criminal imputation, thus realizing the effective allocation of risk responsibility and the reasonable imputation [271, 272]. Objectively, in the complex and detailed AI industrial process, the general attribution of harmful results to a certain subject in fact does not meet the demands of imputation for negligence crime involving AI. Therefore, only by determining the risk responsibility allocation between different subjects in the criminal imputation, can the problem of imputation for negligence crime involved in AI be reasonably solved.

The premise for people to participate in the social interactions is that they have the obligation to ensure that the sphere of his risk responsibility does not present any risk that harms the legal interests of others. Therefore, each person has his own sphere of risk responsibility. For the perpetrator, the result of the realization of his risk can be attributed to him only if his behavior creates a risk prohibited by law within his scope of risk responsibility. In the imputation for negligence crime involving AI, effective allocation of risk and reasonable attribution of liability can only be achieved by judging the legally impermissible risk created by the perpetrator in accordance with the theory of risk responsibility.

3.4.3 *Realization of Risk Within Scope of Norm Protection Purposes*

The fact that the act creates a risk that is not permitted by the law merely opens up the possibility of the criminal imputation. Only when the risk is realized in reality, that is, when the risk realizes the result of endangering the validity of the norm, the attribution of responsibility for the act is only possible. It follows that the result achieved by the risk is a prerequisite for the attribution of responsibility to the perpetrator. However, the key question is whether the risk created by the perpetrator should be attributed to the perpetrator as long as that result is realized in the reality. This is what the following section will concentrate on.

Purpose Scope of Normative Protection

A risk created by the perpetrator as a result of a breach of his duty of care can only be determined to be realized if the risk is realized in a result that is within the purpose scope of normative protection. Thus, the norm protection purpose is a prerequisite for determining whether the risk is realized in the result [94, 273]. In criminal law theory, the purpose of normative protection was originally a subordinate concept of risk realization, but now this concept is much more used to illustrate an important concept of objective attribution theory [173, 274]. Today, with the general prevention purpose of punishment, much more theories advocate considering the purpose of normative protection as a theoretical basis for understanding the risk realization in the objective attribution theory [100, 108].

For the realization of the risk prohibited by law, the purpose of normative protection is precisely to avoid the consequences of the realization of this risk. In other words, only if the risk is related to this normative protection purpose can the realized result be regarded as the work of the perpetrator through a breach of his duty and thus be attributed to the perpetrator. In order to prevent the realization of special constitutive elements of a specific crime, any risk that gives rise to the realization of that constitutive elements should be the risk prohibited by law, and therefore any behavior that contributes to the realization of that risk is also prohibited by the norm. For the perpetrator, there is a connection between the normative purpose of care and the norm realization [88, 89]. In fact, the purpose scope of normative protection serves to limit the boundary for attributing responsibility to the perpetrator. Therefore, the mere fact that the risk is realized in the result does not mean that this result must be attributed to the perpetrator. In this regard, it is also necessary to determine whether the result of risk realization falls within the purpose scope of normative protection [186, 194].

However, how can we determine the purpose of normative protection? The key here is to determine whether there is a consistent purposive correlation between the constitutive elements that are realized and the norm that avoids the realization of the constitutive elements of a specific crime. As far as criminal law norms are concerned, the legislator conveys to the citizens by describing the constitutive elements of a specific crime that behavior fulfilling the constituent elements is prohibited, otherwise it will be punished by criminal law. In terms of the norm function, norms used to describe the constitutive elements of crime belong to the behavioral norm, while those that determine the penalties to be imposed on the perpetrator belong to the punitive norm. Thus, criminal law norms consist of behavioral norm and punitive norm [275, 276]. When attributing the responsibility for the result of the risk realization, whether the result is within the protective purpose of the norm is in fact a determination of whether the punitive norm is a risk prohibited by the behavioral norm. Of these two kinds of norms, the punitive norm for negligence crime is clear and certain, so how to clarify the behavioral norm for negligence crime involving AI becomes crucial in determining the purpose of normative protection [78, 277].

In modern society, due to the rapid development of science and technology, the trend of complexity, specialization and refinement in the field of public management has continued. For the industries with higher risks, in order to prevent and control the technical risks, the government has formulated a large number of detailed laws and regulations, and industry associations have also established numerous regulations. These special norms developed in society to regulate and constrain the specialized activities within the industry are the main elements in determining the duty of care in the norms of conduct for negligence crime [278, 279]. However, in determining the purpose of normative protection, such particular norms are only the basis for identifying the behavioral norm. Therefore, such purpose is still determined by the behavioral norm in the negligence crime.

For the perpetrator, the result of the risk created by him can be attributable to him only if it is realized within the purpose scope of normative protection. If the risk is realized in a result that is outside this scope, the criminal attribution should be excluded to the perpetrator. How can it be determined that the risk has realized within the scope of the normative protection? In this regard, it is important to first identify what factors cause the risk to realize in the result, and then to analyze what measures can effectively prevent the occurrence of this harmful result [140, 158]. Finally, it should be determined whether these measures are part of duty of care owed to the perpetrator. If these corresponding measures are a duty of care incumbent on the perpetrator, the result of the risk realization is within the purpose scope of normative protection, and therefore the result should be attributed to the perpetrator, otherwise, the realization of the risk contradicts the protective purpose of the norm and thus precludes the attribution of the responsibility for it [26, 100].

For example, a person injured in a car accident died of a bacterial infection while being treated in the hospital. In that example, the behavioral norm, which is relevant to the death from the bacterial infection, is the safety rules of the medical process, but not the traffic safety regulations that were violated by the person who caused this traffic accident. In other words, there is no correlation in purpose between the behavioral norms violated by the perpetrator and the norms of the medical safety. Therefore, the perpetrator of the traffic accident cannot be penalized for the death of the victim from his bacterial infection. It follows that the relevance of the behavioral and punitive norms in terms of purpose does not depend on the general preventive purpose of the punitive norms, but rather on the security purpose of a particular legal interest. This specific purpose can be determined by the risk itself, the specific relationship between the perpetrator and the victim [70, 71, 191].

Normative Duty Violation and Risk Realization

In order to cope with the imputation gaps in the imputation for negligence crime involving AI, the imputation structure has shifted from will to norm imputation, so that the risk created by the perpetrator that is prohibited by law must have been realized in a normative sense in its outcome. In other words, there must be a correlation, in the normative sense, between the act of risk creation and the outcome of risk realization. In a specific case, if the perpetrator complies with his legal duties, the realization of the risk is not caused by his violation of such legal duties, so the perpetrator cannot be attributed the liability for the result. It can be seen that the risk is realized in the result because the perpetrator violated his duty of care. Judging the connection between the creation and the realization of risk in a normative sense is, to some extent, another perspective to argue for the shift in the imputation structure for negligence crime involving AI towards the normative imputation.

According to the previous discussion, the creation of risk prohibited by law comes from the fact that the perpetrator violates this duty of care. Therefore, the key to determining whether there is a normative connection between the risk creation behavior and risk realization result is to determine which factors influenced the actor to violate his duty of care. In this regard, according to some theoretical understandings, it is necessary to normatively replace the conduct of the perpetrator in breach of his duty of care with the conduct in conformity with that duty, thereby determining whether the harmful result will still occur [234, 280]. Essentially, this point of view is to judge whether the result will still occur when the perpetrator performs an act that complies with his duty of care. A normative connection between the creation and the realization of risk can be established if the perpetrator acted in compliance with his duty of care and the corresponding harmful result did not occur.

Therefore, the perpetrator complied with his duty of care and the result did not occur, which shows that his behavior that violated the duty of care played a positive role in causing the result to occur. Once the perpetrator acts in compliance with his duty, the factors that precipitated the result disappear. However, if the perpetrator complies with his duty and the harmful result still occurs, there is no normative connection between the risk-creating act and the result of the realization of the risk. Therefore, the duty of care has decisive significance in whether the harmful result occurs [20, 123, 281].

According to the above discussion, there is no normative connection between the creation of risk and the occurrence of result, as long as the perpetrator complies with his duty of care and the corresponding created risk is not realized in the result. In fact, this is an ideal logic of judgment. In reality, there are a large number of uncontrollable influence factors between the creation of risk and the occurrence of result, from which it is difficult to exclude other factors and ultimately identify the determinants of the results [282, 283]. The connection between the creation of risk and the occurrence of result is often expressed only as a certain causal probability. The key question here, therefore, is to what extent or with what probability the perpetrator's compliance with his duty of care would have avoided the occurrence of the harmful results.

In this regard, one view is that a connection between the risk creation and result realization exists only when the perpetrator complies with his duty of care and the harmful result could definitely have been avoided. In this case, even when the perpetrator complies with his duty of care and there is still a one-percent or even smaller chance that the result will occur, the normative connection should be excluded

[150, 254]. According to this view, the normative connection is a fundamental requirement for the criminal imputation. Therefore, only when it can be determined that the perpetrator's compliance with his duty of care can 100% avoid the occurrence of the harmful results, the normative connection between them can be determined. As long as this normative connection is affirmative and identified, no matter what causal factors exist between the behavior and the result, this judgment of certainty of avoidance can completely eliminate its influence. For the criminal imputation, only by determining this normative connection in the strictest sense can we avoid mistakenly attributing the results in the negligent crime to the perpetrator [140, 284].

In contrast, the other view is that the perpetrator, who has exceeded the risk prohibited by law and realized it, has elevated a prohibited risk. The results caused by the elevation of the risk can still be attributed to the perpetrator [285, 286]. Comparing these two different views, we can find that both views are judged by whether the perpetrator can avoid the result by complying with his duty of care. However, the first view holds that only if this possibility of such result is 100% unavoidable, the normative connection between the two can be positively decided. The second view, however, holds that there is a normative connection between the two, as long as the perpetrator elevates that risk.

Indeed, modern society is full of factors with uncertainties that are difficult to control and reproduce, making it extremely difficult to thoroughly identify the impact and extent of these factors on the occurrence of outcomes when determining such normative connection [287, 288]. Even if it is possible to limit the main factor to the duty violation through the connection between obligation compliance and outcome avoidance, it is still difficult to effectively exclude the influence of other factors on the outcome. In this regard, the avoidance of the result does not exist in the course of the objective judgment, because it is itself a matter of probability. In response to the probability in the normative connection judgments, if we insist that the normative connection can be excluded only if it is 100 percent possible to avoid the occurrence of result, then the criminal imputation should be waived for all the results below that probability. In the case of negligence crime involving AI, it is the existence of a large number of uncertain factors that results in the corresponding outcome. If this view is followed, any imputation for such crime involving AI should be abandoned [289–291]. It can be seen that the view of elevated risk is relatively more reasonable.

However, is the perpetrator liable for the realized result whenever he elevates the risk of his breach of his duty of care? A key question here is, to what extent was the risk elevated before there is a normative connection between the risk creation and the result occurrence. In this regard, most views attempt to develop a detailed probabilistic division between absolute occurrence and absolute non-occurrence, thereby determining the relationship between the degree of the elevated risk and this normative connection [102, 292]. For example, some people believe that if it is not certain whether the same result will occur if the actor complies with the duty of care, then as long as the actor violates the duty of care and brings harm to the object of the action that is much higher than the normal risk, then the result should be attributed to Responsible for the perpetrator. For example, it is not certain whether the same result would have occurred when the perpetrator complied with his duty of care.

In this case, as long as the breach of duty by the perpetrator creates a much higher risk than normal to the object of the act, then the occurrence of result should be attributed to him [111, 293]. In fact, only the result, which occurs as a result of such a significant elevation in risk can be attributed to the perpetrator. In this case, the corresponding result can be avoided with a high degree of probability only if the perpetrator complies with his duty of care.

Risk Realization in Imputation for Negligence Crime Involving AI

In the imputation for the negligence crime, risk realization identifies that the prohibited risk created by the perpetrator is realized in the result, and the significance of the normative connection between risk creation and risk realization for the criminal imputation. It is the risk realization that many problems associated with the traditional negligence crime are avoided in the imputation for this kind of crime. Objectively, verification of the risk realization is important in rationally dealing with the gap in the imputation for negligence crime involving AI.

According to the previous discussion, the negligence crime is predicated on the perpetrator's violation of his duty of care. Generally speaking, in order to ensure the safety of some risky industries, the corresponding laws, regulations, industry rules and other normative documents become the source of the person's duty of care. Therefore, whenever an actor violates the requirements of these special norms, he has possibility to violate his duty of care. Therefore, these special norms determine the scope of negligence crime to some extent. However, with the rapid development and wide application of AI technology, these duties of care that are too strict with the perpetrator have become a negative force that limits and hinders the technological innovation in our society. This is because the development of AI technology is accompanied with much greater uncertainty and risk, so the corresponding more complex and detailed norms will inevitably guide and manage its development and application [170, 294]. In the field of AI, if the duty of care comes from these complicated special regulations and norms, then the scope of negligence crime involving AI will inevitably be unduly expanded. Accordingly, this will undoubtedly increase the obligation burden on the AI designers, producers and other practitioners, and further in fact hinder the development and application of this technology [295, 296].

However, in the imputation for negligence crime involving AI, as the imputation structure shifts from will to the norm imputation, the judgment of attribution of the result to the perpetrator depends on whether the risk he creates is realized within the purpose scope of normative protection. Consequently, the result of the realization of risk created by the perpetrator in breach of his duty of care is not necessarily attributable to him [1, 297]. It is only when the result realization is within the purpose scope of normative protection that the result may be attributed to the perpetrator. It follows that risk realization objectively precludes the attribution of a considerable part of results. These results are the realization of the risk created by the perpetrator beyond the purpose of the normative protection, despite the fact that he has violated these norms. For the negligence crime involving AI, the risk realization objectively limits the scope of such crime.

In the imputation for negligence crime, the connection between the risk creation and risk realization is likewise manifested in the determination of the causality between the behavior and the result. For the traditional imputation for negligence crime, causality is empirically determined at the factual level only through the conditional theory [37, 298]. However, with the rapid development and widespread application of AI technology, this causal process has become increasingly difficult to determine, because a large number of uncontrollable and difficult-to-identify factors play a role in this causal process. In addition, due to the complexity of technology, even those who engage in the development or production of AI technology have difficulty in identifying this causal process in the areas outside their risk responsibility. In this case, the judgment of causality with the traditional theories has made it difficult for this responsibility element to play its proper role in practice [299, 300]. In order to avoid such impact on the imputation for the negligence crime involving AI, the realization of prohibited risk theory seeks to establish a normative connection between the risk creation and risk realization in a normative sense. As argued previously, for determining such normative connection, the theory puts forward the idea of whether the result could have been avoided if the perpetrator had complied with the norm. This theory overcomes the imputation dilemma for the negligence crime by moving away to some extent from an over-reliance on the factual causation.

In the imputation for negligence crime involving AI, if the risk created by the perpetrator with his breach of duty is realized in the result, is the result necessarily attributable to him? With the characteristics of negligence crime involving AI, the traditional imputation theory faces the challenge of unduly expanding the scope of imputation for the risk realization [269, 301]. To this end, the doctrine of elevated risk establishes the plausibility that not all results realized with the prohibited risk created by perpetrator may be attributed, thus providing a reasonable solution to the dilemma of overly broad imputations for this kind of crime involving AI. According to its understanding, if the perpetrator has exceeded the permissible risk, he has not only created a risk that is prohibited by law, but has also realized that risk [96, 176]. The result realized by the perpetrator as a result of the elevated risk by him should be attributed to him.

In the crime involving AI, a large number of uncontrollable and difficult-to-reproduce factors inevitably determine the causal flow of risk realization, which undoubtedly increases the difficulty of identifying the normative connection. Faced with these uncertainties, traditional imputation theory either completely deny or completely affirm that the perpetrators are to be attributed for the realization of the risk [199, 201, 302]. In order to avoid these difficulties in imputation, the elevated risk view establishes that only results that achieved can be attributed to the perpetrator only if he significantly elevated the risk. This undoubtedly opens up the possibility of rationally dealing with the challenges in the imputation for negligence crime involving AI.

Faced with the challenge of imputation for negligence crime involving AI, as the focus of this study, this chapter concentrates on providing a reasonably theoretical systematic frame for this challenge. As a premise, the structure of such criminal imputation needs to shift from will to norm imputation. Accordingly, the unlawfulness is primarily a violation of norms by behavior and its result. As verification in the normative imputation for such crime, its contents include the risk creation as well as risk realization within the purpose scope of normative protection. In this respect, the reasonable delineation of risk responsibility for the perpetrator provides a prerequisite for determining that the perpetrator has created the risk prohibited by law. As long as such risk is realized within the scope in the normative sense, then the risk realization should be attributed to the perpetrator.

References

1. Ulgen O (2021) A human-centric and lifecycle approach to legal responsibility for AI. Commun Law J J Comput Media Telecommun Law 26(2):8832
2. Williams G (2020) Taking Responsibility for Negligence and Non-negligence. Crim Law Philos 14:113–134. https://doi.org/10.1007/s11572-019-09506-8
3. Čerka P, Grigienė J, Sirbikytė G (2015) Liability for damages caused by artificial intelligence. Comput Law Sec Rev 31(3):376–389. https://doi.org/10.1016/j.clsr.2015.03.008
4. Hallevy P (2019) The basic models of criminal liability of AI systems and outer circles. In: The basic models of criminal liability of AI systems and outer circles. https://doi.org/10.2139/ssrn.3402527
5. Ambos K (2006) Toward a universal system of crime: comments on george fletcher's grammar of criminal law. Cardozo L Rev 28:2647
6. Dubber MD (2005) The promise of German criminal law: a science of crime and punishment. German Law J 6(7):1049–1071. https://doi.org/10.1017/S2071832200014127
7. Lagier DG, Lagier DG (2003) The debate in criminal law. Paradoxes Act Hum Act Law Philos 17:39–54. https://doi.org/10.1007/978-94-017-0205-8_4
8. Beiser FC (2009) Normativity in neo-kantianism: its rise and fall. Int J Philos Stud 17(1):9–27. https://doi.org/10.1080/09672550802610941
9. Presskorn-Thygesen T (2017) The significance of normativity: studies in post-kantian philosophy and social theory. Frederiksberg: Copenhagen Business School (CBS). PhD series No. 13.2017
10. Bickhard MH (2014) The social ontology of persons. In: Social interaction and the development of knowledge. Psychology Press, pp 111–132
11. Tissaw MA (2013) The person concept and the ontology of persons. The psychology of personhood: philosophical, historical, social-developmental, and narrative perspectives, pp 19–39. https://doi.org/10.1017/CBO9781139086493.003
12. Jakobs G (2004) Imputation in criminal law and the conditions for norm validity. Buffalo Crim Law Rev 7(2):491–511. https://doi.org/10.1525/nclr.2004.7.2.491
13. Toepel F (2012) The fault element in the history of German criminal theory: with some general conclusions for the rules of imputation in a legal system. Crim Law Philos 6:167–186. https://doi.org/10.1007/s11572-012-9150-4
14. Brink DO (2019) The nature and significance of culpability. Crim Law Philos 13:347–373. https://doi.org/10.1007/s11572-018-9476-7
15. Simester A (2021) Fundamentals of criminal law: responsibility, culpability, and wrongdoing. Oxford University Press, Oxford

16. Behme T (2002) Pufendorf's doctrine of sovereignty and its natural law foundations. In: Natural law and civil sovereignty: moral right and state authority in early modern political thought. Palgrave Macmillan, London, pp 43–58. https://doi.org/10.1057/9781403919533_4
17. Howard JJ (2004) Kant and moral imputation: conscience and the riddle of the given. Am Cathol Philos Quart 78(4):609–627. https://doi.org/10.5840/acpq200478444
18. Battistoni G (2020) Action and imputation between morality and ethical life: hegel. In: Morale, Etica, religione tra filosofia classica tedesca e pensiero contemporaneo. studi in onore di francesca menegoni. Padova University Press, pp 435–455
19. Vieweg K (2020) Hegel's philosophical theory of action. In: The idealism of freedom. Brill, pp 96–114. https://doi.org/10.1163/9789004429277_009
20. Feigenson N, Park J, Salovey P (1997) Effect of blameworthiness and outcome severity on attributions of responsibility and damage awards in comparative negligence cases. Law Hum Behav 21:597–617. https://doi.org/10.1023/A:1024856613829
21. Vdovichen V, Vdovichena L (2019) Professional responsibility of notaries: ontological aspect. Eur J Law Pub Admin 6:148
22. Lou J (2021) Doctrines of causation in Japan. Int J Crim Just Sci 16(2):73. https://doi.org/10.5281/zenodo.4756073
23. Moore M, Hurd HM (2011) The culpability of negligence. Crime Punish Respon Jurisp Antony Duff 18:311. https://doi.org/10.1093/acprof:oso/9780199592814.003.0018
24. Burns K, Bechara A (2007) Decision making and free will: a neuroscience perspective. Behav Sci Law 25(2):263–280. https://doi.org/10.1002/bsl.751
25. Fletcher GP (2017) The theory of criminal negligence: a comparative analysis. The structure and limits of criminal law. Routledge, New York, pp 441–478
26. Husak D (2011) Negligence, belief, blame and criminal liability: the special case of forgetting. Crim Law Philos 5:199–218. https://doi.org/10.1007/s11572-011-9115-z27
27. Bublitz JC, Merkel R (2014) Crimes against minds: on mental manipulations, harms and a human right to mental self-determination. Crim Law Philos 8(1):51–77. https://doi.org/10.1007/s11572-012-9172-y
28. Papacharalambous CN (2022) Criminal law guilt and ontological guilt: a heideggerian perspective. Law Crit 12:1–25. https://doi.org/10.1007/s10978-021-09289-9
29. Mansourabadi A, Mousavi-Asl SS (2022) Criminal behavior, from the teleology of the practical wisdom of tradition to modern mechanism. Public Law Stud Quart 52(2):709–727
30. Rachlin H (2007) Free will from the viewpoint of teleological behaviorism. Behav Sci Law 25(2):235–250. https://doi.org/10.1002/bsl.746
31. Aponte L (2007) Normative gaps in the criminal law: reasons theory of wrongdoing. New Crim Law Rev 10(1):102–141. https://doi.org/10.1525/nclr.2007.10.1.102
32. Simons KW (1994) Culpability and retributive theory: The problem of criminal negligence. J Contemp Legal 5:365
33. Walen AD (2022) On Blame and Punishment: Self-blame, Other-Blame, and Normative Negligence. Law Philos 41(2–3):283–304. https://doi.org/10.1007/s10982-021-09436-4
34. Greenberg A (2021) Why criminal responsibility for negligence cannot be indirect. Camb Law J 80(3):489–514. https://doi.org/10.1017/S0008197321000659
35. Spencer JR, Brajeux M-A (2010) Criminal liability for negligence—a lesson from across the channel? Int Comp Law Quart 59(1):1–24
36. Birzu B (2020) Offenses of service negligence at work: critical opinions. Acta Univ Danub Jurid 2020(2):106–120
37. Berman MN (2022) Negligence and culpability: reflections on alexander and Ferzan. Crim Law Philos 16(3):455–468. https://doi.org/10.1007/s11572-021-09583-8
38. Perin A (2019) When risk management systems 'fail': on criminal negligence and the limits of scientists' responsibility. Ethics Law Chem Biol Radiol Nucl Explos Crises 30:211–225. https://doi.org/10.1007/978-3-030-11977-5_17
39. Güver L, Kneer M (2022) Causation and the silly norm effect. Adv Exp Philos Law 133:47203
40. Boldt RC (1991) Construction of responsibility in the criminal law. Univ Pa Law Rev 140:2245

41. Nachkebia G (2012) The problem of objective imputation in criminal law. J Law 2012(2):250–259
42. van Oosten F (1983) Causation and limitation of liability in german criminal law. Tydskrif vir Hedendaagse Romeins-Hollandse Reg J Contemp Roman-Dutch Law 46(4):383–405
43. Agudelo Molina J (2021) Causation and imputation: the internal coherence of the objective imputation theory in the field of civil liability. Revista de Derecho Privado 41:321–356
44. Langford P, Bryan I (2013) Hans kelsen's concept of normative imputation. Ratio Juris 26(1):85–110. https://doi.org/10.1111/raju.12004
45. Battistoni G (2017) Beyond causality: a reinterpretation of Hegel's concept of Tat in the question of the responsibility and imputation. Pólemos 1(2/2017):82–99
46. Battistoni G (2019) The normative function of the right of objectivity in hegel's theory of imputation. In: Concepts of normativity: Kant or Hegel? Brill, pp 120–140. https://doi.org/10.1163/9789004409712_010
47. Carrino A (2016) Chapter 5 from the criticism of neo-Kantianism to neo-Hegelianism in the philosophy of law. In: A treatise of legal philosophy and general jurisprudence: Volume 12: legal philosophy in the twentieth century: the civil law world, Tome 1: language areas, Tome 2: main orientations and topics. Springer, Dordrecht, pp 189–207. https://doi.org/10.1007/978-94-007-1479-3_5
48. Avrigeanu T (2009) Justification, imputation and punishment. Curentul Jurid Jurid Curr Le Courant Jurid 4:15–37
49. Barzun C (2016) Causation, legal history, and legal doctrine. Buffalo Law Rev 64(1):81–100. https://doi.org/10.2139/ssrn.2714005
50. Solan LM, Darley JM (2001) Causation, contribution, and legal liability: An empirical study. Law Contemp Probl 64(4):265–298. https://doi.org/10.2307/1192298
51. Khiluta V (2021) Free will in criminal law through the lens of neuroscience. J East Eur Crim Law 2021(2):63–72
52. Nestor PG (2019) In defense of free will: neuroscience and criminal responsibility. Int J Law Psych 65:101344. https://doi.org/10.1016/j.ijlp.2018.04.004
53. Puppe I, Grosse-Wilde T (2022) A ness causation-based concept for imputation of harm in criminal law. Univ West Austr Law Rev 49(1):306–343. https://doi.org/10.3316/informit.525760882428947
54. Decker JF (2008) The mental state requirement for accomplice liability in American criminal law. South Carol Law Rev 60(2):237–382
55. Schuster F (2009) Main structures of product liability in german private and criminal law. Stellenbosch Law Rev 20(3):426–453
56. Ohlin JD (2014) Searching for the hinterman: in praise of subjective theories of imputation. J Int Crim Just 12(2):325–343. https://doi.org/10.1093/jicj/mqu004
57. Simester AP (2017) Causation in (criminal) law. Law Quart Rev 113:416–441
58. Hoctor S (2012) General principles and specific offences: recent cases. South Afr J Crim Just 25(3):398–405
59. Mkhize AP (2015) Foresight of the causal sequence as a requirement of dolus eventualis in consequence crimes (Doctoral dissertation)
60. Aires de Sousa S (2022) Connections (and limits) between law and natural sciences: the concepts of causality and culpability from the perspective of criminal law. Int J Semiot Law-Revue internationale de Sémiotique juridique 35(1):287–296. https://doi.org/10.1007/s11196-020-09788-5
61. Chen C (2020) Research on the mechanism of unreasonable objective attribution. In: Proceedings of the 5th international conference on economics, management, law and education (EMLE 2019). Atlantis Press, pp 938–943. https://doi.org/10.2991/aebmr.k.191225.179
62. Cryer R (2014) Imputation and complicity in common law states: a (partial) view from England and Wales. J Int Crim Just 12(2):267–281. https://doi.org/10.1093/jicj/mqu011
63. Kelman M (1981) Interpretive construction in the substantive criminal law. Stanford Law Rev 591–673. https://doi.org/10.2307/1228535

64. Robinson PH (2017) Imputed criminal liability. The structure and limits of criminal law. Routledge, New York, pp 29–96
65. de Sousa MP, Carmo J (2013) A semantic model for causation in criminal law and the need of logico-legal criteria for the attribution of causation. Law Probab Risk 12(3–4):207–228. https://doi.org/10.1093/lpr/mgt005
66. Moughalian GV (2021) Understanding the negligence question. Lincoln Memor Univ Law Rev 9(1):126–186
67. Huigens K (2004) On aristotelian criminal law: a reply to duff. Notre Dame JL Ethics Pub Pol'y 18:465. https://doi.org/10.1007/978-1-349-60073-1_9
68. Primus EB (2017) Federal review of state criminal convictions: a structural approach to adequacy doctrine. Michig Law Rev 44:75–122
69. Garrett BL (2007) Aggregation in criminal law. Calif Law Rev 95:383–450
70. Puppe I (2016) Negligence and responsibility in road traffic. Ingeborg Puppe Eur J Crime Crim Law Crim Just 2:2003
71. Puppe I (2016) The result and its causal explanation in criminal law
72. Ast S (2020) Von der subjektiven zur objektiven Zurechnung–Die Handlungs-und Tatbestandslehre in der Strafrechtswissenschaft der alten Bundesrepublik. In: Strafrecht in der alten Bundesrepublik 1949–1990. Nomos Verlagsgesellschaft mbH & Co. KG, pp 247–262. https://doi.org/10.5771/9783748910862
73. Hübner C (2011) Die Entwicklung der objektiven Zurechnung. Duncker und Humblot 41:1–321
74. Knobe J, Shapiro S (2021) Proximate cause explained. Univ Chicago Law Rev 88(1):165–236
75. Wikström POH (2019) Situational action theory: a general, dynamic and mechanism-based theory of crime and its causes. Handbook on crime and deviance, pp 259–281. https://doi.org/10.1007/978-3-030-20779-3_14
76. Alexander L, Ferzan KK (2009) Crime and culpability: a theory of criminal law. Cambridge University Press, Cambridge
77. Frowe H (2022) Risk imposition and liability to defensive harm. Crim Law Philos 16(3):511–524. https://doi.org/10.1007/s11572-021-09588-3
78. Alicke MD, Rose D, Bloom D (2011) Causation, norm violation, and culpable control. J Philos 108(12):670–696
79. Walters GD, White TW (1988) Crime, popular mythology, and personal responsibility. Fed Probat 52(1):18–26
80. Jakobs G (2008) Norm, person, gesellschaft-vorüberlegungen zu einer rechtsphilosophie. 3. Auf., Duncker und Humblot Verlag
81. Ohana D (2010) Trust, distrust and reassurance: diversion and preventive orders through the prism of Feindstrafrecht. Mod Law Rev 73(5):721–751. https://doi.org/10.1111/j.1468-2230.2010.00816.x
82. Ambos K (2016) Ius puniendi and individual criminal responsibility in international criminal law. In: Mulgrew/Abels research handbook on the international penal system, pp 57–79. https://doi.org/10.2139/ssrn.2801016
83. Pawlik M (2017) Normbestätigung und Identitätsbalance-Über die Legitimation staatlichen Strafens. Nomos
84. Pawlik M (2012) Das unrecht des bürgers. Grundlinien der Allgemeinen Verbrechenslehre. Mohr Siebeck
85. Hallevy G, Hallevy G (2010) The legitimate sources of the criminal norm. Mod Treat Princip Legal Crim Law 542:15–47. https://doi.org/10.1007/978-3-642-13714-3_2
86. Navarro PE, Moreso JJ (2005) Applicability and effectiveness of legal norms. Law Philos 16(2):201–219. https://doi.org/10.1023/A:1005884330974
87. Jakobs G (2011) Strafrecht, allgemeiner teil-die grundlagen und die zurechnungslehre. 2. Aufl., De Gruyter
88. Roxin C, Greco L (2020) Strafrecht Allgemeiner Teil Bd. 1: Grundlagen. Der Aufbau der Verbrechenslehre. 5. Auf., C.H.Beck

89. Roxin C, Greco L (2020) Strafrecht, Allgemeiner Teil, Band I: Grundlagen Aufbau der Verbrechenslehre. 5. Aufl. C.H. Beck
90. Wei L (2019) Legal risk and criminal imputation of weak artificial intelligence. In: IOP conference series: materials science and engineering, vol 490. IOP Publishing, p 062085. https://doi.org/10.1088/1757-899X/490/6/062085
91. Greco L (2021) The method of (German) criminal law dogmatics. In: Methodology of criminal law theory: art, politics or science? Nomos, pp 129–140. https://doi.org/10.5771/9783748904755-129
92. Kuhlen L (2001) Objektive Zurechnung bei Rechtfertigungsgründen. In: Schünemann B, Achenbach H, Bottke W, Haffke B, Rudolphi H (eds) Festschrift für Claus Roxin zum 70. De Gruyter, pp 331–348. https://doi.org/10.1515/9783110877021.331
93. Rengier R (2001) Gedanken zur Problematik der objektiven Zurechnung im Besonderen Teil des Strafrechts. In: Schünemann B, Achenbach H, Bottke W, Haffke B, Rudolphi H (eds) Festschrift für Claus Roxin zum 70. De Gruyter, pp 811–826. https://doi.org/10.1515/9783110877021.811
94. John D (2020) Rechtswidrigkeitszusammenhang und Schutzzweck der Norm. https://doi.org/10.5771/9783748905745
95. Rudophi HJ (1969) Unrechtsbewusstsein, Verbotsirrtum und Vermeidbarkeit des Verbotsirrtums. Verlag Otto Schwartz & Co, Göttingen
96. Schladitz P (2021) Ein modernes System der subjektiven Zurechnung. Juristische Rundschau 2021(10):487–496. https://doi.org/10.1515/juru-2021-0035
97. Höffler K (2023) Strafrechtliche Aspekte der Zwangsbehandlung: Zugleich Überlegungen zur objektiven Zurechnung beim Garanten. Zeitschrift für die gesamte Strafrechtswissenschaft 135(3):489–522. https://doi.org/10.1515/zstw-2023-0020
98. Leu N (2022) Kritik der objektiven Zurechnung. Sui Generis Verlag, p 428
99. Hilgendorf E (2020) Gefahr und Risiko im (Straf-) Recht. Klärungsvorschlägeaus interdisziplinärer Perspektive. In: Gefahr. Nomos Verlagsgesellschaft mbH & Co. KG, pp 9–28. https://doi.org/10.5771/9783845299082-9
100. Ambos K (2020) Goeckenjan, Ingke: Revision der Lehre von der objektiven Zurechnung. Eine Analyse zurechnungsausschließender Topoi beim vorsätzlichen Erfolgsdelikt. Mohr Siebeck, Tübingen 2017. XI, Jus Poenale 13, 331 Seiten. Zeitschrift für die gesamte Strafrechtswissenschaft 132(2):453–469.https://doi.org/10.1515/zstw-2020-0016
101. Haas V (2019) Die objektive Zurechnung beim unechten Unterlassungsdelikt. In: Festschrift zum 70. Geburtstag von Professor Dr. Dr. hc mult. Urs Kindhäuser. Nomos Verlagsgesellschaft mbH & Co. KG, pp 177–192 https://doi.org/10.5771/9783845286266-177
102. Jülich S (2022) Die Diskussion um die Risikoerhöhungslehre. Göttinger Rechtszeitschrift 5(8):29–37
103. Walter T (2022) Zurechnung als Gerechtigkeit: Zugleich Besprechung von BGH 4 StR 19/20 (BASF-Fall), in diesem Heft auf Seite 257. Juristische Rundschau 2022(5):224–231. https://doi.org/10.1515/juru-2022-2124
104. Aichele A (2011) Ex contradictione quodlibet–Die Untauglichkeit der Äquivalenztheorie zur Erklärung von Kausalität, die Untauglichkeit der Lehre von der objektiven Zurechnung zur Rechtfertigung von Zurechnungsurteilen und ein Vorschlag zur Güte. Zeitschrift für die gesamte Strafrechtswissenschaft 123(2):260–283. https://doi.org/10.1515/zstw.2011.260
105. Kindhäuser U (2005) Objektive und subjektive Zurechnung beim Vorsatzdelikt. Jahrbuch Für Recht Und Ethik Annu Rev Law Ethics 13:527–542
106. Aichele A (2017) Zurechnung. In: Hilgendorf E, Joerden J (eds) Handbuch rechtsphilosophie. J.B. Metzler, Stuttgart, pp 401–409. https://doi.org/10.1007/978-3-476-05309-1_57
107. Guanarteme Sánchez Lázaro F (2014) Zur Zurechnung des Erfolgs: prolegomena einer personalen Zurechnungslehre. Zeitschrift für die gesamte Strafrechtswissenschaft 126(2):277–304. https://doi.org/10.1515/zstw-2014-0015
108. Schladitz P (2022) Abstraktes Gefahrbewusstsein und die Vorstellung von der konkreten Möglichkeit der Tatbestandsvollendung: Begriffliche Klarstellungen zum Vorsatz: Zugleich ein Beitrag zum Verhältnis von Gefährdungs- und Verletzungsvorsatz. Zeitschrift für die gesamte Strafrechtswissenschaft 134(1):97–148. https://doi.org/10.1515/zstw-2022-0002

109. Schumacher U (2023) Jürgen Wolter zum 80. Geburtstag: Die objektive Zurechnung des Erfolgs—eine Strafrechtstheorie macht Karriere. Juristische Rundschau 2023(9):422–427
110. Kindhäuser U (2023) Strafrechtliche Zurechnung bei subjektiven Zielkonflikten. In: Strafrecht als Risiko. Nomos Verlagsgesellschaft mbH & Co. KG., pp 271–288. https://doi.org/10.5771/9783748929109-271
111. Greco L (2005) Das Subjektive an der objektiven Zurechnung: Zum "Problem" des Sonderwissens. Zeitschrift für die Gesamte Strafrechtswissenschaft 117(3):519–554
112. Nestler N (2019) Die objektive Zurechnung: nur eine Frage der Wahrscheinlichkeit? JURA Jurist Ausbild 41(10):1049–1057. https://doi.org/10.1515/jura-2019-2279
113. Fischer T (2010) Risikomanagement und objektive Zurechnung. In: Lüderssen K, Kempf E, Volk K (eds) Die Finanzkrise, das Wirtschaftsstrafrecht und die moral. De Gruyter, Berlin, pp 190–200. https://doi.org/10.1515/9783899498448.3.190
114. Blöser C (2014) Zurechnung bei Kant: Zum Zusammenhang von Person und Handlung in Kants praktischer Philosophie. De Gruyter, Berlin. https://doi.org/10.1515/9783110366990
115. Shaver KG (2016) An introduction to attribution processes. Routledge, New York
116. Denga M (2023) Zurechnung-vom trennungsprinzip zum mehrebenensystem. Mohr Siebeck 5:351–358
117. Luhmann N (2022) Äquifinalität Zurechnung. In: Schriften zur Organisation 5: Vorträge\ Lexikonartikel Rezensionen. Springer, Wiesbaden, pp 367–376. https://doi.org/10.1007/978-3-658-23434-8_50
118. Alexander L (2019) Reconsidering the relationship among voluntary acts, strict liability, and negligence in criminal law. In: Controversies in criminal law. Routledge, pp 32–54
119. Fordham M (2002) Suicidal prisoners and the duty of care in negligence. Singap J Legal Stud 2002(1):431–443
120. Park RS (2021) Doe v. mckesson: the "duty" of certification and the "risks" of negligent protester standard. Tulane Law Rev 95(4):1009–1028
121. Green L (1961) Foreseeability in negligence law. Columbia Law Rev 61(8):1401–1424. https://doi.org/10.2307/1119989
122. McManus F (2021) Negligence. In: Delict essentials, 4th edn. Edinburgh University Press, Edinburgh, pp 5–50. https://doi.org/10.3366/j.ctv1hm8hh9.6
123. Melia MC (2007) Victims and self-liability in criminal law: beyond contributive negligence and foreseeability (without blaming the victim). Pace Law Rev 28:739
124. Ashworth A (2008) A change of normative position: determining the contours of culpability in criminal law. New Crim Law Rev Int Interdiscipl J 11(2):232–256. https://doi.org/10.1525/nclr.2008.11.2.232
125. Witt J, Savige M (2023) Foreseeability conventions. Cardozo Law Rev 44(3):1075–1142
126. Genschow O, Brass M (2022) Belief in free will relates to attributions of intentionality and judgments of responsibility. Adv Exp Philos Free Responsib 15:13–26
127. Gudjonsson GH (1984) Attribution of blame for criminal acts and its relationship with personality. Person Individ Differ 5(1):53–58. https://doi.org/10.1016/0191-8869(84)90137-5
128. Simmler M, Markwalder N (2019) Guilty robots? Rethinking the nature of culpability and legal personhood in an age of artificial intelligence. In: Criminal law forum, vol 30. Springer, New York, pp 1–31. https://doi.org/10.1007/s10609-018-9360-0
129. Thuis T, Li T, van Heck E (2023) Who takes responsibility for AI? A field study on AI-related task shifts, explainability, and responsibility attributions. https://aisel.aisnet.org/icis2023/aiinbus/aiinbus/3
130. Fillon AA, Strauch L, Feldman G (2023) Evaluations of action and inaction decision-makers in risky decisions resulting in negative outcomes: inaction agents are preferred to and perceived as more competent and normative than action agents. Collabra Psychol 9(1):74817. https://doi.org/10.1525/collabra.74817
131. Morris MW, Larrick RP (1995) When one cause casts doubt on another: a normative analysis of discounting in causal attribution. Psychol Rev 102(2):331. https://doi.org/10.1037/0033-295X.102.2.331

132. Robinson PH, Grall JA (1983) Element analysis in defining criminal liability: the model penal code and beyond. Stanf Law Rev 35(4):681–762
133. Veresha RV (2016) Criminal and legal characteristics of criminal intent. J Adv Res Law Econ 7(21):1881–1890. https://doi.org/10.1108/JFC-02-2016-0013
134. Ghuman A (2018) Elements of crime. Int J Law Manag Hum 1(4):70–87
135. Kärner M (2022) Interplay between European Union criminal law and administrative sanctions: constituent elements of transposing punitive administrative sanctions into national law. New J Eur Crim Law 13(1):42–68. https://doi.org/10.1177/20322844221085918
136. Ambroz M (2004) The normative aspects of guilt in criminal law. Zbornik Znanstvenih Razprav 64:29
137. Greenberg A (2020) Epistemic responsibility and criminal negligence. Crim Law Philos 14(1):91–111. https://doi.org/10.1007/s11572-019-09507-7
138. Whiting R (1991) Negligence, fault and criminal liability. South Afr Law J 108(3):431–452
139. Stanila L (2021) The fulfillment of the compliance obligation by the legal person and the consequences of its infringement from the criminal law perspective. J East Eur Crim Law 2021(1):9–28
140. Hobe K (1995) Objektive Zurechnung, Fahrlässigkeit und Unrechtsschwere bei den erfolgsqualifizierten Delikten. Sozialpädagogik und Strafrechtspflege: Gedächtnisschrift für Max Busch (1922–1993) Professor für Sozial-und Straffälligenpädagogik an der Bergischen Universität Gesamthochschule Wuppertal, pp 253–277. https://doi.org/10.1007/978-3-86226-468-1_12
141. Leonard G (2003) Towards a legal history of american criminal theory: culture and doctrine from blackstone to the model penal code. Buffalo Crim Law Rev 6(2):691–832. https://doi.org/10.1525/nclr.2003.6.2.691
142. Roxin C (2004) Das strafrechtliche Unrecht im Spannungsfeld von Rechtsgüterschutz und individueller Freiheit. Zeitschrift für die gesamte Strafrechtswissenschaft 116(4):929–944. https://doi.org/10.1515/zstw.2004.116.4.929
143. Araujo T, Helberger N, Kruikemeier S, De Vreese CH (2020) In AI we trust? Perceptions about automated decision-making by artificial intelligence. AI Soc 35:611–623. https://doi.org/10.1007/s00146-019-00931-w
144. Makridakis S (2017) The forthcoming artificial intelligence (AI) revolution: its impact on society and firms. Futures 90:46–60. https://doi.org/10.1016/j.futures.2017.03.006
145. Cunneen M, Mullins M, Murphy F (2020) Artificial intelligence assistants and risk: framing a connectivity risk narrative. Ai Soc 35:625–634. https://doi.org/10.1007/s00146-019-00916-9
146. Floridi L, Cowls J, Beltrametti M, Chatila R, Chazerand P, Dignum V et al (2021) An ethical framework for a good AI society: opportunities, risks, principles, and recommendations. Ethics Gov Policies Artif Intell 78:19–39. https://doi.org/10.1007/978-3-030-81907-1_3
147. Scherer MU (2015) Regulating artificial intelligence systems: risks, challenges, competencies, and strategies. Harv J Law Technol 29:353. https://doi.org/10.2139/ssrn.2609777
148. Stuurman K, Lachaud E (2022) Regulating AI: a label to complete the proposed act on artificial intelligence. Comput Law Sec Rev 44:105657
149. Kröger T (2016) Der Aufbau der Fahrlässigkeitsstraftat-Unrecht, Schuld, Strafwürdigkeit und deren Bezüge zur Normentheorie. Duncker und Humblot
150. Preuß W (2021) Untersuchungen zum erlaubten Risiko im Strafrecht. Duncker and Humblot S 161 ff
151. Kraus VB, Blanco FJ, Englund M, Karsdal MA, Lohmander LS (2015) Call for standardized definitions of osteoarthritis and risk stratification for clinical trials and clinical use. Osteoarth Cart 23(8):1233–1241. https://doi.org/10.1016/j.joca.2015.03.036
152. Wade K (2017) Defining the Threshold of Permissible Risk for Non-therapeutic Clinical Trials with Children in Europe. Eur J Health Law 24(4):414–431
153. Hellmann U (2020) Rechtfertigungsgründe. In: Strafrecht in der alten Bundesrepublik 1949–1990. Nomos Verlagsgesellschaft mbH & Co. KG, pp 295–312
154. Lübbe W (1995) "Erlaubtes Risiko" Zur Legitimationsstruktur eines Zurechnungsausschließungsgrunds. Deut Z Philos 43(6):951–963. https://doi.org/10.1524/dzph.1995.43.6.951

155. Hoyer A (2009) Erlaubtes Risiko und technologische Entwicklung. Zeitschrift für die gesamte Strafrechtswissenschaft 121(4):860–881. https://doi.org/10.1515/ZSTW.2009.860
156. Knauer F (2014) Zur Wiederkehr der Sozialadäquanz im Strafrecht-Renaissance einer überholten Rechtsfigur oder dogmatische Kategorie der Zukunft? Zeitschrift für die gesamte Strafrechtswissenschaft 126(4):844–865. https://doi.org/10.1515/zstw-2014-0034
157. Albrecht HJ (1995) Strafe und Prävention: Eine Herausforderung für Rechtswissenschaft und Justiz. Diskurs 5(1):15–22
158. Fateh-Moghadam B (2019) Innovationsverantwortung im Strafrecht: Zwischen strict liability, Fahrlässigkeit und erlaubtem Risiko—Zugleich ein Beitrag zur Digitalisierung des Strafrechts. Zeitschrift für die gesamte Strafrechtswissenschaft 131(4):863–887. https://doi.org/10.1515/zstw-2019-0031
159. Singelnstein T (2019) Fahrlässigkeit und Gesellschaft—kriminologische Befunde zur Bedeutung der Fahrlässigkeitsdelikte im System strafrechtlicher Sozialkontrolle. Zeitschrift für die gesamte Strafrechtswissenschaft 131(4):1069–1104. https://doi.org/10.1515/zstw-2019-0037
160. De Bruycker I, Beyers J (2015) Balanced or biased? Interest groups and legislative lobbying in the European news media. Polit Commun 32(3):453–474. https://doi.org/10.1080/10584609.2014.958259
161. Stratmann T (2002) Can special interests buy congressional votes? Evidence from financial services legislation. J Law Econ 45(2):345–373. https://doi.org/10.1086/340091
162. Meßerschmidt K (2019) Special interest legislation and legislative capture. Concept Misconcept Legisl 30:243–272. https://doi.org/10.1007/978-3-030-12068-9_10
163. Schulze-Fielitz H (2016) Paths towards better legislation, detours and dead-ends. In: Rational lawmaking under review: legisprudence according to the German Federal constitutional court, p 3. https://doi.org/10.1007/978-3-319-33217-8_3
164. Benditt TM (1975) Law and the balancing of interests. Soc Theory Pract 3(3):321–342
165. Zerara AL (2023) The legislative balance between stability and sustainability in the labor market: a study of the United Arab Emirates legislation. Journal of Legal Sciences 38(1):615
166. Ramraj VV (1999) Criminal negligence and the standard of care. Sing J Legal Stud 248:678
167. Tofaris S, Steel S (2016) Negligence liability for omissions and the police. Cambridge Law J 75(1):128–157. https://doi.org/10.1017/S0008197315001002
168. Hudson B (2003) Justice in the risk society: challenging and reaffirming 'justice' in late modernity. Justice in the risk society. SAGE Publications, New York
169. Galaz V, Centeno MA, Callahan PW, Causevic A, Patterson T, Brass I et al (2021) Artificial intelligence, systemic risks, and sustainability. Technol Soc 67:101741. https://doi.org/10.1016/j.techsoc.2021.101741
170. Steimers A, Schneider M (2022) Sources of risk of AI systems. Int J Environ Res Public Health 19(6):3641. https://doi.org/10.3390/ijerph19063641
171. Wright SA (2020) Ai in the law: towards assessing ethical risks. In: Proceedings of the 2020 IEEE international conference on big data (big data). IEEE, pp 2160–2169. https://doi.org/10.1109/BigData50022.2020.9377950
172. Finkelstein C (2002) Excuses and dispositions in criminal law. Buffalo Crim Law Rev 6(1):317–359. https://doi.org/10.1525/nclr.2002.6.1.317
173. Simmler M (2020) The importance of placing blame: criminal law and the stabilization of norms. In: Criminal law forum, vol 31. Springer, New York, pp 147–178. https://doi.org/10.1007/s10609-020-09390-1
174. Chambliss WJ (2011) Crime and criminal behavior. Sage, New York
175. van Alphen E (1993) Kelsen and hruschka: concepts of imputation. Int J Semiot Law 6(2):163–178
176. Lagioia F, Sartor G (2020) Ai systems under criminal law: a legal analysis and a regulatory perspective. Philos Technol 33(3):433–465. https://doi.org/10.1007/s13347-019-00362-x
177. Osmani N (2020) The complexity of criminal liability of AI systems. Masaryk Univ J Law Technol 14(1):53–82. https://doi.org/10.5817/MUJLT2020-1-3
178. Pawar AV (2018) Autopilot, criminal responsibility, and diversion: a case series. Ann Indian Psych 2(2):139–143. https://doi.org/10.4103/aip.aip_44_18

179. Zurkinden N (2020) Trust in the Functioning of Technology and Criminal Liability Based on the Example of Driving Automation. Redes Organ Concepts Connect Soc 12:291–303. https://doi.org/10.1007/978-3-030-27957-8_22
180. Henry N, Powell A (2016) Sexual violence in the digital age: the scope and limits of criminal law. Soc Legal Stud 25(4):397–418. https://doi.org/10.1177/09646639156242
181. Pratt J, Miao M (2019) Risk, populism, and criminal law. New Crim Law Rev 22(4):391–433. https://doi.org/10.1525/nclr.2019.22.4.391
182. Horder J (1997) Gross negligence and criminal culpability. Univ Toronto Law J 47:495
183. Luden H (1847) Handbuch des teutschen gemeinen und particularen Strafrechtes; Bd.1. Jena: Friedrich Luden, pp 228–229
184. Schurz G (2014) Einführung in die Wissenschaftstheorie. wbg Academic, pp 105–106
185. Kuhn OE, Kuhn OE (2014) Attribution von verantwortung. Alltagswissen in der Krise: Über die Zurechnung der Verantwortung für die Finanzkrise 32:39–77. https://doi.org/10.1007/978-3-658-04724-5_3
186. Moore MS (2010) Placing blame: a theory of the criminal law. Oxford University Press, Oxford
187. Irmler M (2021) Strafrechtliche verantwortung. Heilberufe 73(2):45–47. https://doi.org/10.1007/s00058-021-1964-9
188. Simmler, M. (2021). Strafrechtliche Verantwortung im Zeitalter autonomer Technik: Vom Individual-zum Unternehmensstrafrecht? https://www.alexandria.unisg.ch/handle/20.500.14171/110094
189. Weinreb LL (2019) Desert, punishment, and criminal responsibility. In: Criminal law. Routledge, pp 61–94
190. Cardi WJ (2005) Purging foreseeability. Vand. Law Rev 58:739–809
191. Zipursky BC (2014) Reasonableness in and out of Negligence Law. Univ Pennsyl Law Rev 163:2131
192. Fried CS, Reppucci ND (2001) Criminal decision making: the development of adolescent judgment, criminal responsibility, and culpability. Law Hum Behav 25(1):45. https://doi.org/10.1023/A:1005639909226
193. Lacey N (2001) Responsibility and modernity in criminal law. J Polit Philos 9(3):249–276. https://doi.org/10.1111/1467-9760.00127
194. Duff RA (2007) Answering for crime: responsibility and liability in the criminal law. Bloomsbury Publishing
195. Pratt J (2020) Law, insecurity and risk control. Springer, New York
196. Kant I (1974) Metaphysik der Sitten Vigilantius, in: Kant's gesammelte Schriften, hrsg. Von der Akademie der Wissenschaften der DDR, Bd. 27/1, Berlin. 543
197. Grégoire P, Van Oppens H (2006) Risk attribution. J Perform Measur 11(1):67
198. Jagannathan R, Patel SA, Ali MK, Narayan KV (2019) Global updates on cardiovascular disease mortality trends and attribution of traditional risk factors. Curr Diab Rep 19:1–12. https://doi.org/10.1007/s11892-019-1161-2
199. Königs P (2022) Artificial intelligence and responsibility gaps: what is the problem? Ethics Inform Technol 24(3):36. https://doi.org/10.1007/s10676-022-09643-0
200. Santoni de Sio F, Mecacci G (2021) Four responsibility gaps with artificial intelligence: why they matter and how to address them. Philos Technol 34:1057–1084. https://doi.org/10.1007/s13347-021-00450-x
201. Coeckelbergh M (2020) Artificial intelligence, responsibility attribution, and a relational justification of explainability. Sci Eng Ethics 26(4):2051–2068. https://doi.org/10.1007/s11948-019-00146-8
202. Constantinescu M, Voinea C, Uszkai R, Vică C (2021) Understanding responsibility in responsible AI: dianoetic virtues and the hard problem of context. Ethics Inform Technol 23:803–814. https://doi.org/10.1007/s10676-021-09616-9
203. Welzel H (1931) Kausalität und Handlung. Zeitschrift für die gesamte Strafrechtswissenschaft 51:703–720

204. Roxin C (2021) Der Fall Zschäpe: Täterschaft oder Teilnahme? BGH, Beschluss vom 12. August 2021–3 StR 441/20. Juristische Rundschau 2021(12):644–652
205. Roxin C (2022) Täterschaft und Tatherrschaft. De Gruyter, Berlin
206. Schünemann B (2020) Band II Täterschaft als Herrschaft über den Grund des Erfolges. De Gruyter, Berlin
207. Murmann U (1993) Die Nebentäterschaft im Strafrecht-Ein Beitrag zu einer personalen Tatherrschaftslehre. Duncker und Humblot
208. Chesterman S (2020) Artificial intelligence and the limits of legal personality. Int Comparat Law Quart 69(4):819–844. https://doi.org/10.1017/S0020589320000366
209. Hallevy G (2010) The criminal liability of artificial intelligence entities-from science fiction to legal social control. Akron Intell Prop J 4:171. https://doi.org/10.2139/ssrn.1564096
210. Solum LB (2020) Legal personhood for artificial intelligences. In: Machine ethics and robot ethics. Routledge, pp 415–471
211. Coca-Vila I (2018) Self-driving cars in dilemmatic situations: an approach based on the theory of justification in criminal law. Crim Law Philos 12(1):59–82. https://doi.org/10.1007/s11572-017-9411-3
212. Coeckelbergh M (2016) Responsibility and the moral phenomenology of using self-driving cars. Appl Artif Intell 30(8):748–757. https://doi.org/10.1080/08839514.2016.1229759
213. Orr W, Davis JL (2020) Attributions of ethical responsibility by artificial intelligence practitioners. Inform Commun Soc 23(5):719–735. https://doi.org/10.1080/1369118X.2020.1713842
214. Bambauer J (2023) Negligent AI speech: some thoughts about duty. J Free Speech Law 3:343. https://doi.org/10.2139/ssrn.4432822
215. Nakar S, Weinberger S, Greenbaum D (2015) Legal and social implications of predictive brain machine interfaces: duty of care, negligence, and criminal responsibility. AJOB Neurosci 6(4):40–42. https://doi.org/10.1080/21507740.2015.1094558
216. Reed C (2018) How should we regulate artificial intelligence? Philos Trans R Soc A Math Phys Eng Sci 376(2128):20170360. https://doi.org/10.1098/rsta.2017.0360
217. Lidander L, Novakazi F, Erhardsson G (2022) Building blocks of responsibility: a conceptual model illustrating the factors influencing perceived responsibility over the driving task when interacting with driving automation systems. In: Adjunct proceedings of the 14th international conference on automotive user interfaces and interactive vehicular applications, pp 137–140. https://doi.org/10.1145/3544999.3552524
218. Novakazi F, Johansson M, Erhardsson G, Lidander L (2021) Who's in charge? The influence of perceived control on responsibility and mode awareness in driving automation. Inform Technol 63(2):77–85. https://doi.org/10.1515/itit-2020-0020
219. Kurpiers C, Biebl B, Mejia Hernandez J, Raisch F (2020) Mode awareness and automated driving—what is it and how can it be measured? Information 11(5):277. https://doi.org/10.3390/info11050277
220. Milakis D, Van Arem B, Van Wee B (2017) Policy and society related implications of automated driving: a review of literature and directions for future research. J Intell Transp Syst 21(4):324–348. https://doi.org/10.1080/15472450.2017.1291351
221. Leiman T (2021) Law and tech collide: foreseeability, reasonableness and advanced driver assistance systems. Policy Soc 40(2):250–271. https://doi.org/10.1080/14494035.2020.1787696
222. Feldmanis L (2019) The principle of trust for exceptions to the non-regression clause in the case of delict of negligence. Juridica Int 28:86
223. Katz L (2003) Harm and justification in negligence. Theor Inquir Law 4(1):1067. https://doi.org/10.2202/1565-3404.1067
224. Navarro PE, Orunesu C, Rodríguez JL, Sucar G (2004) Applicability of legal norms. Can J Law Jurisp 17(2):337–359. https://doi.org/10.1017/S0841820900003945
225. Schünemann B (2004) The system of criminal wrongs: the concept of legal goods and victim-based jurisprudence as a bridge between the general and special parts of the criminal code. Buffalo Crim Law Rev 7(2):551–582. https://doi.org/10.1525/nclr.2004.7.2.551

226. Plunkett JC (2015) The historical foundations of the duty of care. Monash Univ Law Rev 41(3):716–744. https://doi.org/10.3316/ielapa.058226479407472
227. Smillie JA (1989) The foundation of the duty of care in negligence. Monash Univ Law Rev 15:302–335. https://doi.org/10.3316/agispt.19910422
228. Herstein OJ (2010) Responsibility in negligence: why the duty of care is not a duty "to try." Can J Law Jurisp 23(2):403–428. https://doi.org/10.1017/S0841820900004987
229. Nolan D (2013) Deconstructing the duty of care. Law Quart Rev 129:559–588
230. Raz J (2010) Responsibility and the negligence standard. Oxford J Legal Stud 30(1):1–18. https://doi.org/10.1093/ojls/gqq002
231. Cockburn T, Butler D (2018) Negligence. Health law in Australia, 3rd edn, pp 271–394
232. Granne I, Corfield L (2010) Negligence: the duty of care. Med Law
233. Devereux J, Beran RG (2022) Medical negligence law in Australia. Med Liabil Asia Austr 14:1–12. https://doi.org/10.1007/978-981-16-4855-7_1
234. Pagura I (2015) Negligence: what you need to know. J Austr Tradit Med Soc 21(3):188–190. https://doi.org/10.3316/informit.602613053877177
235. Singh VP, Verma V (2020) Medical negligence: meaning, scope and legal interpretation. Legal Issues Med Pract 161
236. Mulheron R (2020) Principles of tort law, 2nd edn. Cambridge University Press, Cambridge
237. Tofaris S (2018) Duty of care in negligence: a return to orthodoxy? Cambridge Law J 77(3):454–457. https://doi.org/10.1017/S0008197318000831
238. Selbst AD (2020) Negligence and AI's human users. 100 Boston University Law Review 1315
239. Turner J, Turner J (2019) Responsibility for AI. Robot Rules Regul Artif Intell 15:81–132. https://doi.org/10.1007/978-3-319-96235-1_3
240. Abbott R (2020) The reasonable robot: artificial intelligence and the law. Cambridge University Press, Cambridge
241. Kowert W (2017) The foreseeability of human-artificial intelligence interactions. Texas Law Rev 96:181
242. Surden H (2019) Artificial intelligence and law: an overview. Georg State Univ Law Rev 35:19–22
243. Acharya A, Savitha J, Nadagoudar S (2009) Professional negligence in dental practice: potential for civil and criminal liability in India. J For Dent Sci 74:02–07. https://doi.org/10.4103/0974-2948.50880
244. Kashyap S (2022) Medical negligence. In: Health laws in India. Routledge, pp 99–106
245. Vitvitskiy SS, Kurakin ON, Yepryntsev PS, Skriabin OM, Sanakoiev DB (2021) Professional negligence when providing medical care: criminal and procedural aspects. Medico-legal Update 21(3)
246. Brown A (2022) Clinical negligence claims for pressure injuries from the perspective of a tissue viability medico-legal nurse expert. Br J Commun Nurs 27(Sup9):S14–S20
247. Scognamiglio P, Iniziato V, La Pia S, Martiadis V (2023) A no-win situation: psychiatrists navigating competing obligations between free will, paternalism, duty of care, and position of guarantee. Mental Wellness 1(1):4. https://doi.org/10.4081/mw.2023.4
248. Howarth D (2006) Many duties of care—or a duty of care? Notes from the underground. Oxford J Legal Stud 26(3):449–472. https://doi.org/10.1093/ojls/gql014
249. Alexander L, Ferzan KK (2007) Culpable acts of risk creation. Ohio State J Crim Law 5:375
250. González-Vélez AC, Melo-Arévalo C, Martínez-Londoño J (2019) Eliminating abortion from criminal law in Colombia: a just cause. Health Hum Rights 21(2):85–96
251. Henry J (2008) Criminal history on a 'Need to Know' Basis: employment policies that eliminate the criminal history box on employment applications. Just Policy J 5(2):4–22
252. Robinson PH (2003) Prohibited risks and culpable disregard or inattentiveness: challenge and confusion in the formulation of risk-creation offenses. Theor Inquir Law 4(1):1066. https://doi.org/10.2202/1565-3404.1066
253. Stemmer P (2010) Begründen, Rechtfertigen und das Unterdrückungsverbot. Deut Z Philos 58(4):561–575. https://doi.org/10.1524/dzph.2010.58.4.561

254. Kindhäuser U (2008) Risikoerhöhung und Risikoverringerung. Zeitschrift für die gesamte Strafrechtswissenschaft 120(3):481–503. https://doi.org/10.1515/ZSTW.2008.481
255. Sancinetti MA (2008) Risk reduction principle versus importance of results in criminal law theory. InDret 3:6786
256. Bardón CB (2022) Hypothetische Kausalverläufe und Erfolgszurechnung. Goltdammer's Archiv für Strafrecht 169(12):690–705
257. Baunack M (2020) Grenzfragen der strafrechtlichen Beihilfe: unter besonderer Berücksichtigung der sogenannten psychischen Beihilfe. Duncker und Humblot
258. Kaufhold M (2022) Hypothetische Kausalität und Kontrafakten: eine interdisziplinäre Analyse zur Beachtlichkeit von Reserveursachen im zivilen Schadensrecht. Nomos Verlag
259. Goeckenjan I (2017) Revision der Lehre von der objektiven Zurechnung: Eine Analyse zurechnungsausschließender Topoi beim vorsätzlichen Erfolgsdelikt (Vol. 13). Mohr Siebeck
260. Frisch W (2021) Das v. lisztsche straftatsystem: inhalt, erfolgsgeschichte und potentiale. In: Grundlagen und konzepte des strafrechts. Nomos Verlagsgesellschaft mbH & Co. KG., pp 111–152
261. Loewy AH (1987) Culpability, dangerousness, and harm: balancing the factors on which our criminal law is predicated. N Carol Law Rev 66:283
262. Ferrante M (2008) Causation in criminal responsibility. New Crim Law Rev 11(3):470–497. https://doi.org/10.1525/nclr.2008.11.3.470
263. Ahmad MA, Eckert C, Teredesai A (2019) The challenge of imputation in explainable artificial intelligence models. arXiv preprint arXiv:1907.12669. https://doi.org/10.48550/arXiv.1907.12669
264. Stuckenberg CF (2014) Problems of 'subjective imputation' in domestic and international criminal law. J Int Crim Just 12(2):311–323. https://doi.org/10.1093/jicj/mqu023
265. Bavli HJ (2019) Counterfactual causation. Arizona State Law J 51:879. https://doi.org/10.2139/ssrn.3244109
266. Ben-Shahar O (2009) Causation and foreseeability. Encycl Law Econ 1:83–108
267. Güver L, Kneer M (2022) Causation and the silly norm effect. Adv Exp Philos Law 64:133. https://doi.org/10.5040/9781350278301.0015
268. Müller JR, Fischer C (2023) Die strafrechtliche Verantwortung. Die Haftung im Steuer-und Wirtschaftsrecht. Erich Schmidt Verlag GmbH & Co. KG, Berlin, pp 275–536
269. Chaudhary G (2020) Artificial intelligence: the liability paradox. ILI Law Rev. https://doi.org/10.2139/ssrn.3709095
270. Oimann AK (2023) The responsibility gap and LAWS: a critical mapping of the debate. Philos Technol 36(1):3. https://doi.org/10.1007/s13347-022-00602-7
271. Fraser H, Villarino J (2023) Acceptable risks in Europe's proposed AI act: reasonableness and other principles for deciding how much risk management is enough. Eur J Risk Regul 15:1–16. https://doi.org/10.1017/err.2023.57
272. Schuett J (2023) Risk management in the artificial intelligence act. Eur J Risk Regul 45:1–19. https://doi.org/10.1017/err.2023.1
273. Gropp W, Küpper G, Mitsch W (2003) Ein unachtsamer Bauarbeiter und ein gewissenloser Chef. In: Fallsammlung zum Strafrecht. Juristische ExamensKlausuren. Springer, Berlin. https://doi.org/10.1007/978-3-642-55882-5_5
274. Byczyk M (2017) A breach of the norms of cautiousness as fundament for criminal responsibility: a comparative analysis. Eur J Comp Law Govern 4(3):211–245. https://doi.org/10.1163/22134514-00403001
275. Pawlik M (2020) Norm confirmation and identity balance: on the legitimacy of punishing. Crit Anal Law 7(1):34018
276. Simons KW (2002) Does punishment for "culpable indifference" simply punish for "bad character"? Examining the requisite connection between mens rea and actus Reus. Buffalo Crim Law Rev 6(1):219–315. https://doi.org/10.1525/nclr.2002.6.1.219
277. Dancig-Rosenberg H, Feldman Y (2023) A behavioral ethics perspective on the theory of criminal law and punishment. Experiments in moral and political philosophy. Routledge, New York, pp 206–224

278. Begishev I, Khisamova Z, Vasyukov V (2021) From robotics technology to environmental crimes involving robots. In: E3S web of conferences, vol 244. EDP Sciences, p 12029. https://doi.org/10.1051/e3sconf/202124412029
279. Bittle S, Snider L (2015) Law, regulation, and safety crime: exploring the boundaries of criminalizing powerful corporate actors. Can J Law Soc La Revue Canadienne Droit et Société 30(3):445–464. https://doi.org/10.1017/cls.2015.16
280. Witting C (2005) Duty of care: an analytical approach. Oxf J Leg Stud 25(1):33–63. https://doi.org/10.1093/ojls/gqi003
281. Fisse B (1991) The attribution of criminal liability to corporations: a statutory model. Syd L Rev 13:277. https://doi.org/10.3316/agispt.19912904
282. Huigens K (1997) Virtue and criminal negligence. Buff Crim L Rev 1:431
283. Johnson BL (2017) Why negligence per se should be abandoned. NYUJ Legis Pub Pol'y 20:247
284. Miseré CW (2021) Die Grundprobleme der Delikte mit strafbegründender besonderer Folge. Duncker und Humblot, pp 1–183
285. Huber C (2017) Strafrechtliche Verantwortlichkeit von Verbänden verfassungskonform. J Strafrecht 2017(2):129–130
286. Strasser O (2007) Strafrechtliche Verantwortung des Unternehmensjuristen einer Schweizer bank. Nomos Verlagsgesellschaft mbH & Co. KG, pp 749–776
287. Caldwell M, Andrews JT, Tanay T, Griffin LD (2020) AI-enabled future crime. Crime Sci 9(1):1–13. https://doi.org/10.1186/s40163-020-00123-8
288. King TC, Aggarwal N, Taddeo M, Floridi L (2020) Artificial intelligence crime: an interdisciplinary analysis of foreseeable threats and solutions. Sci Eng Ethics 26:89–120. https://doi.org/10.1007/s11948-018-00081-0
289. Beck S (2016) Intelligent agents and criminal law—negligence, diffusion of liability and electronic personhood. Robot Auton Syst 86:138–143. https://doi.org/10.1016/j.robot.2016.08.028
290. Danaher J (2016) Robots, law and the retribution gap. Ethics Inform Technol 18(4):299–309. https://doi.org/10.1007/s10676-016-9403-3
291. La Rosa E (2023) Criminal law and artificial intelligence: which spaces for a criminal liability of the robot? In: Marino D, Monaca M (eds) Artificial intelligence and economics: the key to the future. Lecture notes in networks and systems, vol 523. Springer, Cham. https://doi.org/10.1007/978-3-031-14605-3_14
292. Tag B (2000) Kausalität und objektive Zurechnung. Der Körperverletzungstatbestand im Spannungsfeld zwischen Patientenautonomie und Lex artis: Eine arztstrafrechtliche Untersuchung, pp 391–406. https://doi.org/10.1007/978-3-642-57034-6_16
293. Schömig A (2023) Gefahren und Risiken im Strafrecht. https://doi.org/10.5771/9783748936268
294. Parnas DL (2017) The real risks of artificial intelligence. Commun ACM 60(10):27–31. https://doi.org/10.1145/3132724
295. Hupont I, Micheli M, Delipetrev B, Gómez E, Garrido JS (2023) Documenting high-risk AI: a European regulatory perspective. Computer 56(5):18–27. https://doi.org/10.1109/MC.2023.3235712
296. Jacobs M, Simon J (2022) Assigning obligations in AI regulation: a discussion of two frameworks proposed by the European Commission. Dig Soc 1(1):6. https://doi.org/10.1007/s44206-022-00009-z
297. De Cremer D, Kasparov G (2022) The ethical AI—paradox: why better technology needs more and not less human responsibility. AI Ethics 2(1):1–4. https://doi.org/10.1007/s43681-021-00075-y
298. Giannini A, Kwik J (2023) Negligence failures and negligence fixes: a comparative analysis of criminal regulation of AI and autonomous vehicles. In: Criminal law forum. Springer, Dordrecht, pp 1–43. https://doi.org/10.1007/s10609-023-09451-1
299. Lehmann J, Breuker J, Brouwer B (2005) CAUSATI O NT: modeling causation in AI&law. In: Law and the semantic web: legal ontologies, methodologies, legal information retrieval, and applications, pp 77–96. https://doi.org/10.1007/978-3-540-32253-5_6

300. Lehmann J, Gangemi A (2007) An ontology of physical causation as a basis for assessing causation in fact and attributing legal responsibility. Artif Intell Law 15:301–321. https://doi.org/10.1007/s10506-007-9035-3
301. Kirpichnikov D, Pavlyuk A, Grebneva Y, Okagbue H (2020) Criminal liability of the artificial intelligence. E3S Web Confer EDP Sci 159:04025. https://doi.org/10.1051/e3sconf/202015904025
302. Kiener M (2022) Can we bridge AI's responsibility gap at Will? Ethical Theory Moral Pract 25(4):575–593. https://doi.org/10.1007/s10677-022-10313-9

Chapter 4
Main Conclusions and Future Prospects

AI has become a constitutive element of our human society, and its technology not only has rapidly empowered the economic and social development, but also raised many legal and ethical issues that are highly relevant to the characteristics and development of AI technology itself. In the field of criminal law, the gap created in the imputation for negligence crime involving AI poses the challenge to the traditional imputation theory. It is for this reason that this study attempts to provide a reasonable imputation system for the negligence crime involving AI.

With the description for the characteristics of AI, it can be determined that crime involving AI has owned the characteristics that are different from those of the traditional crimes. Since AI does not have the possibility of taking criminal responsibility as a subject in the criminal law, the unprecedented challenges encountered by the traditional theories in responding to this kind of crime are mainly reflected in the imputation for this crime. Such challenge manifests itself primarily in the gap created by the criminal imputation for the negligent crime involving AI. In regulating crime involving AI in accordance with the traditional criminal law theory, this imputation gap arises because part of the criminal liability cannot be attributed to the appropriate subject. As a result, some subject who should take criminal responsibility escape from assuming it, while certain criminal liability is imposed on subjects who do not need to bear it. However, this imputation gap will not be encountered in all the crimes involving AI. In the intentional crime involving AI, AI is always only a criminal tool, the imputation for such crime can be reasonably dealt with through the theory of error or indirect perpetration in the criminal law theory. Accordingly, the imputation gap for crime involving AI is mainly found in the negligent crimes.

It is mainly because of the characteristics of this crime that the imputation gap only arises in the case of negligence crime involving AI. To a certain extent can AI achieve its autonomy, which in its applications weakens the ability of relevant person to foresee the consequences of his behavior. In addition, AI technology creates an intricate connection between the behavior and the result, which affects the determination of causality in its legal sense. Finally, the corresponding supervision and

S. Zhao, *Principle of Criminal Imputation for Negligence Crime Involving Artificial Intelligence*, Artificial Intelligence and the Rule of Law,
https://doi.org/10.1007/978-981-97-0722-5_4

management regulations related to AI technology have not yet been well established, so such many blank norms hinder the person from judging his duty of care. All this has resulted in a large number of phenomena that do not conform to the traditional cognitive experience cannot be included in the theoretical framework of imputation for negligence crime, which objectively affects the reasonable imputation for such crime.

In order to avoid the impact of some imputation factors on the imputation for negligence crime involving AI, some theoretical efforts have been made to directly determine the criminal liability of relevant persons by establishing the strict liability in the general part of criminal law. In line with this, some views advocate addressing these imputation issues by directly stipulating some negligence crimes involving AI in the specific part of criminal law, such as adding the crime of illegal use of AI and the crime of major safety accidents involving AI. In contrast to this view, other views hold that, despite the many impacts and challenges brought about by AI technology, it has not caused the disruptive impact and influence on the traditional criminal law theory. Therefore, this viewpoint advocates that AI should be regarded as the subject of criminal liability, thereby giving it the possibility to bear the criminal responsibility for his crime committed with its own will. At the same time, if AI commits a crime jointly with a person, the division of their criminal liability should also be considered.

However, with the rapid development and wide application of AI technology, the foreseeability of perpetrator in the negligence crime involving AI has become more and more abstract, and it is also increasingly difficult to determine the causality between the behavior and its result. This has undoubtedly led to various challenges in the imputation for such crime, and has created the gaps in its criminal imputation. In order to rationally address these challenges as well as to bridge the imputation gaps, a shift in the imputation structure from will to norm imputation is a rational choice for the imputation for negligence crime involving AI. In this context, this study attempts to provide a reasonable imputation system for negligence crime involving AI to deal with the criminal imputation gap, which is also the focus of this study.

In this system of attribution, as long as the perpetrator has created a risk that is not permitted by the law, and that risk is realized within the purpose scope of the normative protection, then that result should be attributed to him. Therefore, the creation of risk that is not allowed by the law and the realization of results within the purpose scope of normative protection are the key to dealing with the gaps in the imputation for negligence crime involving AI. However, not all the result, which was realized as a result of the risk created by the perpetrator, should be attributed to him. Only if a prohibited risk is created within the boundary of his risk responsibility, the result can be attributed to the perpetrator. Moreover, the result attributed to the perpetrator must also be one that is within the purpose scope of normative protection, and there is the connection between risk creation and the risk realization in the legal sense.

Undoubtedly, the gaps in the imputation for negligence crime involving AI are only a very specific manifestation of the many challenges that AI has brought to people. Today, as AI has become a constitutive element of our human society, the application of it has the profound and dynamic positive and negative impacts on societies, environment, ecosystems and human lives. In our increasingly divided society today, although the development and application of AI technology will undoubtedly be of great help to mankind and benefit all countries, it can embed and exacerbate, potentially resulting in discrimination, inequality, digital divides, exclusion and a threat to cultural, social and biological diversity and social or economic divides. In addition, AI technologies have also the potential impact on human dignity, human rights and fundamental freedoms, gender equality, democracy, social, economic, political and cultural processes, scientific and engineering practices, and so on. Regarding the development of AI technology, there is the inescapable fact that AI technologies can deepen existing divides and inequalities in the world, within and between countries. For the technologically advanced countries, they will take various measures to restrict the sharing and exchange of AI technology in order to maintain their technological leadership, thus exacerbating the technological gap between different countries.

In the face of this technology, which is deeply changing the fundamental direction of human social development, how can the risks and ethical concerns it poses be reasonably addressed without hindering its innovative development? To this end, the normative framework regulating AI technologies and their social impacts should be based on human consensus and common goals. At the same time, ethical values and principles are linked to the challenges and opportunities associated with AI technologies on the basis of fundamental freedoms, ethics, information and knowledge, and freedom of research and innovation. However, the first problems that need to be confronted include the paradoxical conflicts generated by innovation, asymmetries access to knowledge and technology, as well as barriers to access to information, barriers to access to technological innovations, and the lack of appropriate physical and digital infrastructures and regulatory frameworks.

Only when AI technology pays attention to human dignity and basic freedoms, adheres to cultural diversity and inclusiveness, and adheres to basic ethics and morals, can AI technology develop in a responsible direction. In this context, dealing with the challenges brought about by the imputation for negligence crime involving AI is actually a matter of ethical concern for AI technology with the base of human dignity and freedom.

The manufacturer's authorised representative in the EU is Springer Nature Customer Service Centre GmbH, Europaplatz 3, 69115 Heidelberg, Germany. If you have any concerns regarding our products, please contact ProductSafety@springernature.com

Printed and bound by CPI Group (UK) Ltd, Croydon, CR0 4YY
30/09/2026
02225264-0007